# Film & TV Tax Incentives in the U.S.

Entertainment tax incentives are one of the greatest tools in the arsenal of filmmaking. They pay a portion of production expenditures back to the filmmaker, while creating powerful economic engines for the states who implement them properly. They are high in the list of considerations for executives to sign off before a movie receives the go-ahead for production, even to the point of dictating the location of where a production is filmed. Yet, they are misunderstood by the filmmakers who use them, the politicians who create them, the economists who measure them, and even the scholars who study them. This book puts all the pieces together in a comprehensive look at how the entertainment industry works, how it uses incentives, and how incentives can benefit a filmmaker – or a state.

**Daniel Wheatcroft**, a 25-year voting member for the Oscars, is a veteran of the entertainment industry whose career spans the production, marketing, and distribution of some of Hollywood's biggest success stories. As an Executive at Universal Pictures, he successfully orchestrated marketing campaigns, strategic planning, and talent development for over 200 major motion picture campaigns, including *Jurassic Park*, *Schindler's List*, *Backdraft,* and *Apollo 13*. While at Universal he also formed public relations campaigns for major artists such as Tom Cruise, Arnold Schwarzenegger, Steven Spielberg, and Nicole Kidman.

His production credits include Executive Producer, Producer, and/or Director of 10 network television specials, 125 broadcast features, 180 world premieres, and ShoWest, as well as pioneering the use of new media in the entertainment industry. Well known in the industry for his creative deals, he has developed joint ventures with corporate giants such as Warner Bros., Paramount, Sony Pictures Entertainment, Walt Disney Corp., Universal, Fox, MSN, NBC, CBS, ABC, General Motors, Coca Cola, American Media, and Pepsi.

Wheatcroft held the position of President of the National Association of Theatre Owners of Cal/Nev and ShoWest, the world's largest motion picture industry entertainment convention, representing the creative and technical interests of all major studios, theatre owners, and talent. He was a founding member of the team who launched KEEN/INGENIO, a successful internet company that merges telephony with the internet (now owned by AT&T holdings).

Wheatcroft founded Shoot To Thrill Productions, LLC (STTP), a company that specializes in the development, production, and marketing of entertainment properties. Investors, state governments, corporations, and private entities utilize STTP to connect them to entertainment business opportunities. Clients include Walt Disney Corporation, ABC Studios, Sony Pictures Entertainment, Warner Bros., DreamWorks, Fox Entertainment, Paramount Pictures, Microsoft, Ingenio Corporation, AT&T, and Apple. STTP associates produce a variety of entertainment projects.

Wheatcroft has lectured at the University of Southern California (USC) and has taught classes at The University of Alabama and at Birmingham-Southern College. He has published academic papers in international journals on the economics of film tax incentives and regularly speaks at conferences. He has been a voting member of the Academy of Motion Picture Arts & Sciences since 1993.

**Glenda Cantrell, Ph.D.**, teaches classes in film production management and motion picture marketing at The University of Alabama. She has won the two top teaching awards in her college, the “Board of Visitor’s Excellence in Teaching Award” and the “Kappa Tau Alpha Commitment to Teaching Award.” Her research has been published nationally; her areas of expertise include media marketing and promotion, and entertainment tax incentives. She received both her B.A. and M.A. from the University of Montevallo, and her Ph.D. from The University of Alabama.

Dr. Cantrell is the past President of the Board of Directors for the Broadcast Education Association (BEA). BEA is the international professional association for professors, industry professionals, and graduate students who are interested in teaching and research related to electronic media and multimedia enterprises. She is also the former Chair of the Department of Telecommunication and Film at The University of Alabama.

Before turning to teaching as a career, Dr. Cantrell was the Director of On-Air Promotion at the Eternal Word Television Network (EWTN). Additionally, she was a freelance writer and producer for more than 30 years, working with clients both in the Birmingham, Alabama market, and in the Dallas–Ft. Worth, Texas area.

## Routledge Studies in Media Theory & Practice

1. **Semiotics and Title Sequences**
   Text-Image Composites in Motion Graphics
   *Authored by Michael Betancourt*

2. **Synchronization and Title Sequences**
   Audio-Visual Semiosis in Motion Graphics
   *Authored by Michael Betancourt*

3. **Title Sequences as Paratexts**
   Narrative Anticipation and Recapitulation
   *Authored by Michael Betancourt*

4. **The Screenwriters Taxonomy**
   A Collaborative Approach to Creative Storytelling
   *Authored by Eric R. Williams*

5. **Open Space New Media Documentary**
   A Toolkit for Theory and Practice
   *Patricia R. Zimmermann and Helen De Michiel*

# Film & TV Tax Incentives in the U.S.

## Courting Hollywood

**Glenda Cantrell and Daniel Wheatcroft**

Routledge
Taylor & Francis Group
LONDON AND NEW YORK

First published 2018
by Routledge
2 Park Square, Milton Park, Abingdon, Oxon, OX14 4RN

and by Routledge
711 Third Avenue, New York, NY 10017

*Routledge is an imprint of the Taylor & Francis Group, an informa business*



*Library of Congress Cataloging in Publication Data*
A catalog record for this book has been requested

ISBN: 978-1-138-48968-4 (hbk)
ISBN: 978-1-351-03710-5 (ebk)

Typeset in Times New Roman
by Out of House Publishing

This book is dedicated to the industry professionals who provided guidance along the way; to the filmmakers and dreamers who paved the way for incentives; and to the students who will follow in their footsteps

# Contents

# Preface

"Putting the cart before the horse." This figure of speech dates back as early as 106 BC and refers to someone doing things out of order – or even reversing the expected order.[1] For example, as academics, students, and even the general public, when we think of the path to becoming a filmmaker we think of lights, sound, camera, actors, crew, directors, producers, writers, editing, etc. In other words, we think of the physical production side of filmmaking – "the cart." So we teach about how to make the cart, how to paint the cart, who to put in the cart, what the cart sounds like, where the cart is going, who is going to see the cart, etc. But this scenario, even though it is the "sexy" part of the business, doesn't "pull" itself. Without the money to make the cart, what we learn or teach has no output and becomes meaningless to our goal. Also, without a return on investment, those who provide us with the money will dry up and our dreams will go with it.

What is missing in too many discussions is "the horse," the economic engine that provides the power to the cart – the money that allows us to move a project forward. This book provides the reader with the "reins," or the information on film and television tax incentives – one of the greatest tools in the arsenal of filmmaking. While incentives are not the entire financial "horse," they play an increasingly larger role in the economics of making movies. These incentives can reimburse a portion of production expenditures back to the filmmaker, boosting their production budget, while at the same time creating powerful economic engines for the states who implement them properly. Yet, they are often misunderstood by the filmmakers who use them, the politicians who create them, the economists who measure them, and even the scholars who study them. This book puts all the pieces together – the economics, politics, business, and production management – to provide an in-depth look at how business and production co-exist in film and television, how they use incentives, and how incentives can benefit a filmmaker – or a state.

*Film & TV Tax Incentives in the U.S.: Courting Hollywood* was born out of personal experience. Our research was from the inside out, not from the outside in. Between the two of us, we spent years trying to explain the film industry to politicians or the need for incentives to our students. We researched articles from economists that dismissed industry incentives, overlooking the money spent in a state or the jobs lost when the incentives – and the production – left the state. In our frustration, we discovered there was no one place to use as a reference; no single work that explained both sides of the equation. Finally, we decided that we would be the ones to tackle the subject.

This book is not meant to be a reference for specific incentives offered by each state. Those decisions can change in the blink of an eye, and there are websites that do a great job of keeping up with that information. Instead, this book examines which incentive approaches have worked and which have not; how politicians help and hurt; what we can learn from past successes and failures. Other topics include assessing the value of the entertainment industry to a state, measuring the success of an incentive program, attracting production, and injecting union/guild considerations into a right-to-work state.

Because of the myriad of misconceptions about film tax incentives, this book will be controversial to some. States and politicians who have misused these incentives, or economists who have measured their effectiveness with outdated tools, will no doubt take exception to some of these pages. But this book is intended to put incentives in the context of the entertainment industry – from both the business side and the production side – and demonstrate why the production incentives are significant. It is a handbook for politicians, lobbyists, and other people who want to use filmmaking as an economic growth area. For filmmakers, it is an introduction to another tool for movie making: incentives can be the difference between raising enough money – or shelving your project for another year.

Film & TV tax incentives are a big piece of the filmmaking puzzle. Gaining a better understanding of how those pieces fit together is crucial to the process: for states, policy makers, filmmakers, and students alike. Pick up the reins, and let film tax incentives be the economic engine they were intended to be.

## Note

1 "Put the Cart before the Horse". (n.d.). *The Phrase Finder*. Last accessed November 20, 2017. www.phrases.org.uk/meanings/put-the-cart-before-the-horse.html

# 1 Making Movies?

## Why Entertainment?

An actual conversation between an industry professional and a sitting governor highlights the major problem faced today by entertainment incentives: "So, we're here to talk about making movies?" the governor asked, as he sat back in his chair and grinned. "No," the producer replied. "We're here to talk about business."

This is the classic misconception many politicians have about movie and television production. Most people think immediately of the "movie stars," the creativity, the storytelling involved in filmmaking. Very few people think of movies as a *business*, an industry that creates a product to sell. Those involved in "show biz" contribute to this misconception because it suits them to do so – they want the public to believe in the stories and glamour. It sells more tickets.

Indeed, the film and television industry has fascinated Americans for more than 100 years. Yet while they have followed the industry through fan magazines, newspapers, radio, and now the internet, their actual knowledge of the industry and how it works is very limited. Most people, when they think about film or television, think only of the glamour: major actors or stars, writers, and directors. In reality, the entertainment industry is made up of nearly 89,000 businesses, many of which are small independent companies, and involving hundreds of different skill sets. It is a business and an industry – but unlike any other business on earth.

According to the Motion Picture Association of America (MPAA), the entertainment industry is located in every state of the country. In 2015, the industry supported more than 2 million jobs in the U.S. alone, generating more than $134 billion in wages.[1] This is part of the reason numerous states have sought access to this industry, looking to take part in the work of Hollywood. But there are other reasons that make film-making an appealing draw for states looking to boost their bottom line. The entertainment industry is a mobile, green industry that provides jobs for the trades, new college graduates, and white-collar professions, while simultaneously creating support businesses that can benefit a state.

## Types of Jobs

While the "glamour" jobs of Hollywood are obvious to most, the "nuts & bolts" jobs are more hidden. On any set, there is a need for carpenters, electricians, make-up artists, hair-stylists, caterers, accountants, and more. These "invisible" jobs are the lifeblood of production, and are the key to making incentives work within a state. While many of the crew chiefs will travel from Los Angeles to be supervisors, incentives are only effective if the majority of the crew can be hired locally. The key to establishing the entertainment industry in a state, then, is a combination of the right incentive amount and building a highly trained workforce. Where does this workforce come from?

### *Retrained Labor*

Many states have successfully developed retraining programs to help unemployed workers shift over to the entertainment industry. Carpenters can learn how to apply their skills to building sets instead of homes. Electricians can learn how their trade applies to on-set lighting. Workers trained in hair styling or make-up can advance into applications for the camera. Seamstresses and tailors can assist in sewing costumes or working wardrobe on set, which consists of alterations, repairs, and care of costumes. The art department for a production uses people trained in house painting, interior design, graphics, and other trades in order to create the on-set worlds. The tech industry can learn new applications for their skills as computers, robotic controls, and computer-generated images (CGI) are used in more and more productions. In short, many tradespeople already in a state can find a career resurgence, and good salaries, in the entertainment industry.

### *College Students*

Every state in the U.S. has at least one college or university offering courses in media production. Exact numbers are hard to track, however, because there is not a single common name as with other majors, such as English or history. Schools can establish various monikers such as media production, film production, computing technology, digital production, computer animation, television production, interactive entertainment, mass communication, creative media, motion pictures, or broadcasting. Their goal, however, is the same: turn out students capable of creative leadership on a film or television production. These students fulfill the industry roles for production assistants, writers, production managers, cinematographers, directors, and producers. While some of these graduates will find work in commercial ventures within their own state, the majority will move out of their current state into a place where the entertainment industry is flourishing. Besides Los Angeles and New York, which have always been entertainment centers, graduates now have the option of states such as Georgia, Louisiana, New Mexico, and Ohio, all of which are newer epicenters for production. States without incentives – or without the strong industry presence – find their college graduates moving away to find better jobs. This loss contributes to an economic decline; tax dollars were spent to educate these students from K-5 up. As they become tax-contributing citizens themselves, those contributions now go to support another state.

Whatever it's called, these production programs are a "hot" major. With a generation literally raised on creating their own media content, the gravitation toward this major is easy. Additionally, many high schools now have media production added to their curriculum, giving students the opportunity to try it before they arrive in college. Combined, U.S. colleges and universities turn out thousands of entertainment-ready graduates each year. Their ability to contribute to the economy depends on where they establish their career.

### *Support Businesses*

The support businesses, or vendors, that spring up around the entertainment industry can also contribute greatly to the local economy. While these will be discussed more in Chapter 5, most of them fall into three distinct categories: catering, equipment rental, and props.

Union regulations require that crews be fed, be fed regularly, and be fed well. A well-fed crew is a happy crew, is the Hollywood saying. Hot meals are part of the expectations, and are provided by catering companies that specialize in providing on-set food. These companies support jobs through cooking, delivering, and serving; they also support the local economy through purchasing food and beverages.

For equipment rental, many outsiders don't realize that studios don't provide cameras or sound equipment. Each production, which is usually set up as a limited liability company (LLC), rents its own camera or cameras, lights, sound, cranes, dollies, etc. Equipment rental houses are usually one of the first support businesses to open up in a new market, and provide on-going economic support to a community through jobs and taxes.

Props warehouses are eclectic and can vary from general to specific. Props are considered to be anything an actor touches or moves – from glasses and cups to bicycles and cars. Prop houses usually offer items for rent or purchase, and can also assist with "expendables" – props that are used up during each take. Some businesses focus on a specific specialty area, but most tend to be broad-based. Prop houses support the economy through jobs – floor clerks and purchasing agents – and through sales taxes.

### *Finance, Insurance, and Legal*

Some of the best white-collar jobs in the entertainment industry are the ones no one thinks about. Every entertainment production has at least one accountant. Every production requires multiple layers of insurance. Rental warehouses for props and equipment use insurance. Productions need attorneys to set up LLCs and negotiate contracts. Bank accounts are often set up locally, and some finance is sought at the local level. A certified public accountant (CPA) will be needed to audit the production after completion, especially if incentives are sought. These white-collar jobs and their necessity will be discussed further in Chapter 9.

## Mobility

In most cases, the entertainment industry is not restricted to one place within a state. Unlike other industries, which build a factory or require a specific location, production of movies and television can happen anywhere within a state and can move from location to location. One movie, then, can film in multiple locations, bringing an economic boost to many different areas. Production areas are not limited to metropolitan areas, either; small towns and open natural areas are often utilized for film locations. Additionally, states with varied natural resources – especially mountains, ocean, lakes – can draw in even more production to more areas. This ability to spread production dollars over an entire state can be very appealing.

Weather can be a factor in these decisions, but less than one would think. While the most successful states have a southern climate – specifically, Georgia and Louisiana – film crews are willing to work in any temperature if the work is there. Ohio has been growing as a "destination" state, and Michigan was very successful at luring production despite its colder climate (at least, until their state government shut down the incentive program).

For states without diverse topography, the mobility factor can still exist, but is more tempered. Many of these states, such as New Mexico, have compensated for that by creating large soundstages for production. Although this keeps the filmmakers more centralized, the state does also offer outdoor locations that are perfect for many specific looks.

In short, a mobile industry that does not have to stay in one place within a state can be a positive economic engine.

## Green

In addition to being mobile, the entertainment industry is also a clean industry. There are no factories, no emissions, and no pollution. Through an initiative led in part by the Producers Guild of America (PGA), most studio productions have embraced "Green Filmmaking," a sustainable approach that helps measure any environmental impact or carbon footprint created by a production.[2] Green concerns include items such as local transportation, use of utilities, and fuel used by the production. A website provides a "best practices" guideline for being green, a carbon calculator to assess output, and an online resource for locating green vendors. Professional crews also recycle and clean up their location after a shoot. The green approach means that a state will not generate additional clean-up costs from the filmmaking industry, a claim many other industries cannot make.

## Why Entertainment Incentives?

In today's competitive market place, film and television production relies on entertainment incentives more than ever. While incentives were once included as an afterthought, now incentives are one of the early driving factors in selecting a location. A production with studio backing may even be required to shoot in specific locations in order to obtain incentives and offset some of the cost. Thanks in part to the growth of computer-generated imagery (CGI), it is easier than ever to make one location look like somewhere else entirely. Through the "magic" of location managers and production designers, editors, and effects staff, virtually any script can be shot anywhere and look realistic. Additionally, some scripts are simply re-tooled to take place in a specific setting or location that is more incentive friendly.

For the states that offer incentives, the goal needs to be industry development and job creation. This means creating a competitive incentives plan, writing industry-friendly regulations, and courting the studios that oversee production locations. All three must be in place to build the industry in a state. Otherwise, a state will see only an occasional production – which is not enough to create on-going jobs. Without a concentration of a skilled, trained workforce, the incentives are less desirable since the production company must bring in the entire workforce – a costly endeavor.

To build up this workforce (crew) in a state, at a minimum, productions must be lined up one after another like an assembly line in a factory. This is one of the reasons why the film office needs to be aggressive and knowledgeable in recruiting production. As one production leaves, or "wraps," another production begins. A single production hires hundreds of different individuals; a trained workforce can be hired by many different production companies each year. Thus, even though these crew members are independent contractors, they become a sustainable workforce which can be measured. This is a very important point for the politicians and helps solidify an ongoing incentive program. Additionally, more productions means a higher level of industry presence. A higher level of industry presence creates more jobs and also creates more support businesses. As the crew base grows, the state can handle multiple productions at a time. Multiple productions hire exponentially more crew – and thus the industry is built in the state. Therefore, incentives help build a new economic engine for the state.

Unfortunately, too many states have given up on entertainment incentives before they have had the chance to grow the industry – or, by not understanding how the industry works, have not correctly measured the economic impact. This will be discussed more in Chapter 6. Other states have only courted "easy" productions such as music videos or reality shows. While these types of productions are certainly part of the industry, they have shorter production cycles and smaller crews. Typically, then, a focus on short-term productions does not build out the industry and wastes incentive money without seeing a return on investment. These pitfalls will be discussed in Chapter 7.

Other states have made the mistake of assuming that film and television productions need their state regardless of incentives. Nothing drives the entertainment industry out of a state faster than politicians arrogantly assuming that once the industry is created there it won't leave. The mobile aspect of the industry, while helpful within a state, creates a death knell when incentives are no longer offered. Michigan learned this the hard way; even Los Angeles, the world capital of the entertainment industry, proved no match for incentives in other states. After losing more than $1 billion a year in production,[3] even Hollywood had to re-vamp their incentive program in order to stay "runaway production." With today's high cost of production, incentives are often the primary reason to select a specific location. Chapter 4 will examine more about the impact of the political climate on incentives.

## Conclusion

Movie and television production is a business-based endeavor. Although seen as a "glamour" industry, entertainment actually consists of thousands of businesses of all types – skills and trades, white collar, college graduates, and entrepreneurs – working together to create a "product" that is popular throughout the world. The entertainment industry is both green and mobile, making it an advantageous economic boost for a state. In order to attract this industry, however, a state must have the right incentives in place. This will be discussed in Chapter 2.

## Notes

1 MPAA report. "The Economic Contribution of the Motion Picture & Television Industry to the United States." Prepared in January 2017 based on latest data available (2015). Report released in February 2017.

2 For more information, see the "Green Production Guide" created by the Producers Guild of America. Accessed February 5, 2018. www.greenproductionguide.com

3 "Film L.A. Inc. 2013 Feature Film Production Report". (2014, March 6). *FilmLA.com* Last accessed January 10, 2017. www.filmla.com/wp-content/uploads/2017/08/2013-Feature-Production-Report-w-Release-030614_1394125127.pdf

# 2 Understanding Entertainment Incentives

Entertainment tax incentives, sometimes called film tax incentives, are used to recruit media productions to a specific state or country. Canada first highlighted the drawing power in 1997 when they launched the first comprehensive entertainment tax incentive program. Their success in luring production away from Los Angeles led the state of Louisiana to implement their own tax incentive program in 2001. Other states followed suit; although the numbers vary from year to year, as many as 44 states have offered entertainment incentives at one time or another.

## Qualifying Productions

Incentive applications and disbursement are usually handled by the state Film Office or Film Commission. The details for what qualifies, however, are usually set up by the state legislature or one of the legislative committees. These vary greatly, from state to state but also from year to year. The website run by Entertainment Partners offers the most up-to-date information on each state. Generally speaking, however, there are areas that most states address in funding incentives.

### *Type of Production*

The first consideration is type of production.[1] Every state accepts film production; most states accept scripted television production, and many offer separate applications for television pilot versus television series. No state currently offers incentive money for news, sports, or adult films; infomercials are rarely included. Beyond these, the type of production accepted can vary greatly; potential categories include reality television (unscripted), game shows, talk shows, video games, animation, documentaries, webisodes, commercials, and music videos. Each state determines which type of production qualifies for the incentive.

***Budget***

The second consideration is budget. Most states have a minimum qualifying "spend," i.e., how much money the production will actually spend within the state. Each state also dictates what constitutes as a "qualifying expenditure" toward this spend. In most cases, this spend includes resident labor, equipment rental (camera, lights, sound, etc.), hotel, lumber, food, and fuel; all must be spent with a state-based vendor. Some states also include airfare, if booked through an in-state travel agent, and insurance, if purchased within the state. A few include legal fees if an in-state attorney is used. The expenditures are all subjected to an audit; the qualifying expenditure total is then multiplied by the credit percentage offered by the state to determine what the incentive benefit will be to the production company. Most states also have a spending cap, both on the incentive program and on individual productions. Once a production hits their spending cap, they are not eligible for any more than that amount. This guarantees that one production doesn't utilize an entire year's worth of incentive funds.

Production budgets are also divided into two areas: above-the-line (ATL) and below-the-line (BTL). ATL is the fixed costs: main actors, director, script. BTL costs are those that are paid by the day or by the week; this includes the crew, equipment rentals, food, etc. Many states offer different incentive percentages based on ATL (usually lower) and BTL (usually higher). Again, most of these formulas focus only on a percentage of in-state spend.

***Shooting Days***

A third consideration for most states is the number of shooting days. For a production to create local jobs, they need to spend more than a few days within a state. Some states have a specific number of days that the production must shoot within the state. Other states focus on the overall percentage of shooting days, mandating that a certain percentage of the entire production schedule must be in state. Other considerations reward the different stages of production; most states only award incentives for actual production days, when the entire cast and crew is filming. Some states, however, allow incentive applications for development (writing the script, casting, pre-planning) or post-production (editing, CGI, special effects).

***Additional Notes***

Many states also require their film logo in the end credits of a production. Since industry professionals always watch the credits, this logo aids the state as a marketing tool. Georgia, for example, has been extremely successful with their iconic, full-color peach logo; it stands out, and reminds decision-makers that Georgia has a robust entertainment industry. A few states also apply additional incentive percentages to productions that aid education, either by accepting college interns, or by sending cast/crew members to colleges as guest speakers.

The application process also varies from state to state. Most states have a funding year; this may be based on the calendar year or on the state fiscal year. Most states require that the application be approved before principal photography begins; some states require the application be approved as much as 120 days before production begins. In either case, most states only count qualifying expenditures as those taking place *after* the application is approved. Some states also require that the film office approve the script before the application can be processed, although this is no longer as common as it used to be. In most cases, this is done to ensure that the state will not be put in a bad light or be embarrassed by the film. However, this practice has led to complaints of censorship, and therefore has been eliminated in many states.

## Types of Incentives

There are three types of entertainment incentives offered in the U.S.: tax credits, rebates, and grants. Grants are the least common; they are paid directly from the government to the production. No state tax liability is required, so they are easy for an out-of-state production to use. Rebates, used by only a few more states than grants, are also paid directly to a production company. State tax liability varies; otherwise, grants and rebates are very similar. Both are based on a percentage of qualifying expenditures and are used most often by states that do not collect state income tax.

The most common type of incentive, however, is the tax credit. This is a payment toward, or a direct offset of, the production company's state tax liability. It is also a percentage of qualifying expenditures within the state, like the grant and the rebate, but is not a cash transaction. Most of these credits are also "refundable," meaning that the production company can receive the credit even if they are determined to have no state tax liability. In that case, the company can usually implement the "carry forward" clause, which allows them to hold onto the credit for anywhere from three years to ten years (depending on the state). They can then apply the credit to future production.

Many states allow for transferable tax credits, which are preferred by the studios. This means that a production company with no state tax liability can sell the credit to a taxpayer, broker, or company that *does* have a tax liability. The buyer does not have to be an entertainment company – and in most cases, is not. The credits are usually sold, or brokered, for a percentage of their face value; the production gets cash for their budget, and the purchasing company uses the credits to lower their tax liability. Some states limit the number of allowable transfers, while others do not. Transferable tax credits are preferred by many filmmakers, large and small, because even if they have no tax liability, they will still see financial benefit by selling the credits. If the production has no tax liability, however, and the credits are not transferable, then the incentives are useless except for the possible carry forward – which they may not be able to use. Many of the major studios will not work in states where the tax credits are non-transferable.

## Other Incentives and Perks

Most states focus on only one of these primary types of incentives, although there are a few that have more than one program. Also, many states offer additional perks in an effort to recruit productions. These include exempted or decreased sales tax, and exempted or decreased lodging tax. These agreements only apply to state taxes; however, some counties, cities, or towns will also lower their local taxes as a way to bring production to their area. Sales tax, and especially lodging tax, can mount up quickly for a production, so this incentive can certainly sway a producer or studio executive. States also offer other enticements, such as free office space, fee-waivers for location shoots, and sometimes even grip trucks or equipment. States looking to make the most of their incentive program, and build the local entertainment industry, take the competition between states seriously.

Having a good incentive program, however, is just the start. In order to build out this industry and be successful, a state has to actively pursue the right projects. The most important next step is developing an understanding of how the entertainment industry actually works. This will be discussed in Chapter 3.

## Note

1 See Chapter 7 for the pros and cons of each type of production.

# 3 Understanding the Entertainment Industry

Once upon a time, movie studios made movies. In today's Hollywood, however, it's more accurate to say that movie studios *participate* in the production of movies. Their primary role is now in marketing and distribution. Gone are the days where a studio had total control over their stars, writers, and directors. Today's Hollywood is a more collaborative venture. Studios do still wield enormous clout, but not in the way most movie-goers think. For proper use of entertainment incentives, however, it's important to understand exactly how the film and television industry work.

Most films are divided into two categories: studio films or independent films (indies). The primary difference between these two comes down to money. Studios have access to multiple ways of providing capital for a film. Independent producers must raise their own. This chapter will further explore how each of these productions gets made.

## The Studio Structure

A studio today is a massive business. Half rental facility, half corporate structure, studios have most of what a production company needs to make a film. They rent out soundstages, sets, and back lots; studios also have office space, props, wardrobe, and access to some crew members. They can provide these things at no charge to a favored client in order to get a movie made – or they can charge large amounts for the rentals.

As already noted, however, the biggest asset a studio brings is the ability to raise funds for a production. Studio backing can persuade multiple investors to come on board; a simple look at the opening credits of a studio film can show exactly how many production companies contributed to the budget. Multiple investors help to dilute the risk inherent in filmmaking. Additionally, while studios can and do invest their own funds, they also have other options available to them.

As a distributor, a studio raises funds based on the perceived value of the film. This is often determined by research: public awareness of the project, appeal of the stars or director attached to the film, and popularity of the overall story. The studio then "pre-sells" the film to various audiences using this research. Pre-sales includes international theaters, television (including cable and satellite), streaming services, home DVD sales, and even airline entertainment systems. Occasionally, a film will "pay" for production costs on pre-sales alone, lowering the risk that the studio will lose money. International markets have become increasingly more important in recent years, with big-budget (or "tent-pole" movies) depending heavily on foreign markets to offset their budget.

Because studio films have a distribution deal in place, films with studio backing are more likely to be seen by more people than independent films. Although even a studio film can go straight to DVD, many independent films get no distribution at all.

Studio films are always union films. Even if a production takes place in a right-to-work state, union rules still apply if a major studio is attached. The studio has multiple representatives, however, who will help the producers and production managers with negotiations, contracts, and fringe payments. This is another benefit for being a studio-backed production.

Marketing for a studio film is handled by the studio marketing department. This includes everything from movie posters (called "one sheets"), to trailers, commercials, magazine ads, and billboards. If a movie receives Oscar "buzz," this department will create an Academy campaign, including "screeners," to make sure Academy voters are aware of the film. A social media presence is required in today's culture, so an official website will be created, along with any other social media deemed appropriate for the targeted audience: Facebook, Twitter, Instagram, etc. Some movies lend themselves to contests or social media games, which are also created by the studio marketing department. The marketing department will also hold the movie premiere, schedule talk-show interviews for the stars, and get entertainment news articles published in numerous outlets. In short, the marketing department is responsible for "opening the film" – getting as many viewers into theaters on opening weekend as possible. This is the movie's best chance to be successful and turn a profit. Most studio-backed films receive the full benefit of the marketing department's expertise; the expense, which usually matches the production budget, is carried by the studio, not the producers. However, the studio gets paid back from the box office receipts before any profit is shown.

Most studio marketing departments also have separate divisions to handle other revenue-enhancing possibilities: merchandising and product placement. Product placement is negotiated before a film goes into production; for creative purposes, the products involved must seem organic to the process and story. The production crew must then make sure that the contract is met correctly during production and post-production. Merchandising is a separate category, involving everything from T-shirts to toys. Any "kid's meal" tie-in must be established well in advance of the movie premiere and coordinated with the fast-food company. Other items, including toys for a children's movie, must be designed and manufactured to roll out with the movie. Timing is critical. Both merchandising and product placement can generate income for the film budget.

The benefits of being a studio film are enormous. The distribution and marketing alone are a tremendous investment that a filmmaker alone could not achieve. The downside, however, is that a studio expects to have some involvement in the production of the film. This means having a studio representative, usually a line-producer, help oversee the production budget. The studio can be involved in decision-making, even determining shooting location based on the availability of entertainment incentives. Finally, the studio will check in regularly to determine if the production is on schedule and on budget. Some directors and producers work well in the studio environment while others chafe under the microscope. A few top directors will even fight the studio throughout the production. All in all, however, being backed by a studio is a quicker way to a profit.

### *Determining Profit*

On the other hand, profit for a movie is very difficult to determine. While the total for the production budget is usually released to the public, the marketing budget is not. Industry experts note that the marketing budget is almost always equal to the production budget, and costs can escalate even more if an Oscar campaign is launched. The studio is responsible for "prints" – the copies of the film that are sent to the theaters – and advertising (sometimes called P&A) as outlined previously. All of these costs must be returned to the studio before a profit can be claimed. Although the press is quick to point out the box office gross each week, the public doesn't register the fact that only half of that gross is returned to the studios or filmmakers. Theater owners garner the first payment. A complicated formula is used, based on the number of weeks a film is in the theater, but the general understanding is that the theater owner or chain receives half of the gross.[1] The other half of the box office gross goes back to the studio; investors are paid back, actors who negotiated a payment off the front are paid, marketing costs are paid. Anything left is profit. This process led to the "Rule of 4" as dubbed by the studios – a movie must make four times the amount of its production budget to be considered making a profit. In reality, only a few films reach this measure each year. Studios depend on the ones that do. By spreading costs across multiple pictures and multiple investors, studios can better balance out costs and profits.

## Independent Films

Independent pictures don't have that luxury. By definition, independent pictures, or indies, are films produced outside of the major film studio system. They have lower budgets, fewer (or no) investors, and no distribution deal in place. The filmmakers generally are making a film they believe in, hoping that it will get picked up for screening at film festivals and, ultimately, picked up for distribution. Indies have no guarantee that their picture will be seen by an outside audience.

The growth of film festivals in the 1990s led to a new type of independent filmmaking. Numerous small studios were born, such as Miramax and New Line Cinema; they followed the pattern set by the big studios, but on films with smaller budgets. They created a smaller distribution deal with a smaller marketing budget, but were able to support high-quality films. The scripts attracted top-level actors as well, who previously had avoided independent films. Their success opened the floodgates for independent filmmaking; even the Oscars began paying attention. Eventually, the major studios even opened their own independent branches, with studios such as Fox Searchlight Pictures and Sony Pictures Classics. This type of conglomerate "indie" studio has more in common with the traditional studio than with the true independent pictures.

The "true" indies are dependent on the filmmaker raising the money to produce the film. Some have famously collected cans for recycling or taken part in medical experiments to raise the money.[2] Most, however, hit up family and friends, and have traditionally depended on donated goods and services. In recent years, internet "crowdfunding" has become a popular way for young student or independent filmmakers to raise the needed capital. Most of the funds are donated, not invested, as the filmmakers have no assurances that the film will make any money at all. Donated goods can include food for the crew, costumes or make-up, and even locations. Independent filmmakers not only have smaller budgets, but must stretch their budget as far as possible.

Once the film is complete, the independent filmmaker must create a marketing package to introduce the film. Social media and the internet have made part of this easier; however, they also must budget for printed promotional cards to give out at film festivals. If their film is selected for screening at a major film festival, the filmmakers will need to hire a PR firm in order to make the most of the opportunity.

Film festivals are the lifeblood of independent filmmaking, but have their own set of challenges. Currently, there are more than 3,000 active film festivals in the world; more than 200 are in the U.S. alone. These range from very small, niche festivals to very large festivals that draw industry professionals who are looking for new filmmakers. In North

America, these larger festivals include Sundance, Telluride, Tribecca, SXSW, and Toronto. The drawback is that the larger festivals also receive the most entries, usually in the thousands. The festival can only select enough programming for their venue space – so being selected is prestigious, but very, very difficult. The festivals all charge submission fees as well, which can range from $40 to $110 per entry. Most independent filmmakers must pick and choose carefully which festivals are a good fit for their production. Then, if selected, the filmmaker must pay their own travel expenses to attend the festival (attendance is usually a requirement if the film is selected).

Being selected for screening at a large festival is prestigious; winning an award at a large festival is the pinnacle. This ensures that the film will receive a longer life and a bigger viewing audience, especially if the critical acclaim is positive. This also gets Hollywood's attention, which can lead to a distribution deal. There are two approaches to these deals: a distribution rights agreement or a negative pickup. For a distribution rights agreement, the filmmaker retains the rights over his or her film but agrees to give the distribution company the rights to put the film in theaters. This agreement usually includes U.S. distribution rights, but can also include international distribution rights and/or ancillary markets such as DVD sales. Each of these rights can be negotiated together, separately, or even with different companies. The distribution rights can be a profit-sharing model, where the filmmakers and distribution company each receive a percentage of the profits, or it can be a leasing arrangement, where the distribution company pays a fixed amount for the rights. Each model has its benefits and drawbacks; the distribution company and the filmmaker must each decide what the potential box office gross will be and which model will be most beneficial in that particular circumstance.

For a negative pickup on an independent film, however, the studio actually buys the "negative," or print of the film, and the filmmaker severs all rights to the film. The studio now owns all rights to the film, for both distribution and creative decisions. The amount agreed on is the final amount the producer will receive for the film.[3] Most filmmakers recognize that this is usually not the best deal for their film, but sometimes this will allow them to make their next film and begin building a pedigree.

## Other Considerations

An independent film may be union or non-union, depending on the budget and where the production takes place. If the producers choose to go union, they are responsible for negotiating the contracts and fringes with the union representatives. In the past, very few independent films could afford to be union; new agreements, however, have opened the door for low-budget films – and even low, low-budget films – to become signatory productions. Being union allows the production to hire more experienced crew and provides an easier path to distribution. It also opens the door to hiring professional actors through their own union, the Screen Actors Guild (SAG-AFTRA). Many top-tier actors have participated in signatory independent films in recent years, even working for scale at times, just for the opportunity to work on a film project that speaks to them. SAG actors are not supposed to work on non-union projects; however, the production can apply for an exception under the low-budget provisions.

## Limited Liability Company

In addition to the studio system and the world of independent filmmakers, it is important to understand the use of limited liability companies (LLCs) in the entertainment industry. LLCs are used in two different ways: to organize a business surrounding a film, or to organize a business around a specific individual(s).

The majority of film productions organize as an LLC around the film they expect to make. An LLC provides liability protection for the individuals involved, is flexible for gains and losses, and provides favorable tax benefits. Additionally, there are limited federal guidelines for governance – the LLC is run by the controlling party or parties; in this case, usually the producer(s). State regulations vary. The LLC, then, develops the project, hires the crew and the actors, handles insurance, payroll, and all the numerous expenses generated by a production. Individual investors, corporations, other LLCs, and other production companies can become a member of this LLC and contribute financially into it. After production, it is customary for the film LLC to be dissolved after a final audit is completed.

Almost 100 percent of the crew and talent hired by a production company are considered self-employed by the Internal Revenue Service (IRS). They receive form 1099 at the end of the year from the production LLC. Most crew members or talent, then, will form their own individual LLC for tax purposes and to reduce liability. As an example, although the media may report that an actor is paid $20 million for a film, the money isn't paid directly to the actor. Instead, the production company LLC pays the actor's LLC. The actor's LLC "employs" the actor and accepts the payment for contracting or "renting" the actor for the production. The actor's LLC then uses the payment to pay expenses, taxes, overhead, guild dues, and "salary" to the actor. A crew member's LLC works much the same way. Overall, whether cast or crew, the LLC provides a more favorable tax structure and, especially for crew, a more structured income.

## Subsidies versus Incentives

Because of the structure of the entertainment industry, it is important to recognize the purpose of entertainment incentives as opposed to entertainment subsidies. Incentives are generally designed to bring in companies from outside the state, to generate new jobs within a state, and to create a new industry within the state. Incentives work best, then, when offered to outside productions. When incentives are first introduced into a state, however, a major mistake is offering the incentives primarily to small productions produced by in-state companies. Since these companies are already doing business in the state, and have their employees already in house, this use of incentive money does nothing to build up the industry or create new jobs. What was meant as an incentive actually becomes a type of subsidy.

The exception to this is California. After years of losing production to other states and countries, dubbed "runaway production" by the locals, California had to address the problem in order to keep Hollywood at the center of entertainment. Too many jobs were going out of state, and millions of dollars were being lost due to entertainment incentives in other places. By revamping their incentive program, California was able to stem the tide and keep more production jobs and money at home.

## The Industry and Incentives

How does understanding the industry help states with entertainment incentives? This understanding is key to attracting the right projects, building an industry, and making the most of a state's incentive dollars. Why? When courting Hollywood, it's important to keep the studio system in mind. The distribution agreement is extremely important; having other filmmakers see your location on the screen helps motivate them to seek you out. Films that are shot with incentive money but never seen outside of a film festival do nothing to generate interest in your state. Several states, such as Georgia and New York, even use a visual logo in the credits to increase awareness.

Working successfully with a studio production, whether film or television, is one of the quickest ways to build up the industry within a state. The studios are a small universe, and although competitive, the production heads also talk to each other. A positive experience with one studio can lead to another studio also taking a chance with your state.

A state film office that wants to work with a studio production, however, needs to understand the expectations of the studio. The studio wants a state film office liaison available 24/7 to assist with any problems that may arise while filming. Time is money during production, and, since most film crews work a minimum of 12-hour days, the studio expects someone from the state to be available as well. Some of the studios expect the incentive money to be set aside in a separate bank account, available after the final audit, but guaranteed so that the state cannot promise it elsewhere. The studio will also expect help with locations, permits, local crew, and sometimes local talent. States that cannot deliver will lose out on studio productions. Even worse, some studio productions will only stay in a state long enough to qualify for the incentives, and then move on to a more favorable location for the remainder of the shoot. This costs the state on several counts: in addition to loss of incentive funds, this approach does nothing to create jobs or build the industry. The production usually brings in their own crew, cast, and equipment. The production gives the film office a nice, local press-op, but nothing else to show for the investment.

Independent films also often absorb incentive dollars without contributing to the growth of the industry. A true indie film needs incentive money, but usually has a very small budget. When an indie "crews up" or casts locally, they are usually looking for volunteers, not offering paid positions. They depend on local merchants to donate goods and services, and rarely generate any tax income for the state. With no distribution deal in place, the film could be created yet never shown to an audience. Once a state has created the industry within its borders, some incentive money can be set aside for true independent projects. But courting only independent filmmakers is not the way to build jobs within a state.

An indie backed by a minor studio, or an indie that has a distribution deal in place, is less risky for a state than a "true" independent. These films don't have the same expectation for support that the bigger studio films have, but the filmmakers do expect more support than a true indie. Generally union, these productions have a slightly larger budget and a more professional approach. Best of all, with a distribution deal already in place, there is an excellent chance that the film will be seen by an audience.

Understanding the LLC structure is also very important for measuring the effectiveness of incentives. The entertainment industry, as noted in Chapter 1, is made up of hundreds of small businesses. When the industry settles into a state, these are the people who buy homes and cars, pay taxes, and generally contribute to the economic growth of a state. Because they don't have "full-time jobs," however, as defined by the IRS, these success stories are often not counted when measuring the effectiveness of incentives. Some crew members may work on six separate films within one year; they make a good living, but the work is only counted as "part-time" because each shoot lasts only a short time. Recognizing the structure of the industry is vital to understanding its success.

## Courting Hollywood

Most of all, if a state is to be effective at attracting and building the entertainment industry, the state film office must actively pursue the studios and production companies. It is no longer enough to have good incentives and a nice location. The film office must demonstrate knowledge of the industry, ability, and a willingness to work with the studio system. The head of the film office must be carefully chosen for their industry knowledge and contacts; a political appointee with no background in production is the worst approach for a state. Networking, making connections, and actively marketing a state is vital to success. Attending the location manager's show is nice, but the studio production executive is actually the one who makes the final call. A film office must also recognize that, despite the industry's size and power, Hollywood is really a small town. People talk. One bad experience within a state; one broken promise; one unreturned phone call can stifle the production atmosphere for years – or prevent the industry from growing. But handled correctly, the entertainment industry can be a vital source of economic growth for a state.

## Notes

1 Ebert, R. (2012, March 6). "How Your Ticket Price is Divided." Last accessed February 2, 2017. www.rogerebert.com/letters/how-your-ticket-price-is-divided
2 "Robert Rodriguez Biography." *IMDB.com*. Last accessed February 2, 2017. www.imdb.com/name/nm0001675/bio?ref_=nm_ov_bio_sm
3 A negative pickup can also be arranged by a studio *before* a film is made, with the money paid after the film is completed. The studio gets creative control and all distribution rights, but avoids paying salaries and union fees. The producer must find "gap funding" from a bank or other investor, to be repaid once the film is complete and given to the studio. A negative pickup must be completed on time and on budget for the producer to receive the funds.

# 4 The Political Climate

Politics are always at the heart of entertainment incentives. The state legislature is responsible for passing a bill to create the incentives, although a separate group is often responsible for passing the regulations surrounding them. There are numerous problems with having the government in charge; the biggest pitfalls are misunderstanding the goal, turning incentives into a partisan political hot button, and the potential for corruption.

## Misunderstanding Incentives

Few politicians really understand how the entertainment industry works – and even fewer make an effort to understand it. Many are seduced by the glamour; they envision movie stars and high-profile directors having dinner with them and thanking them profusely for their investment. They see themselves having cameo roles in films, or turning their children into actors. They think everyone associated with the movie business is extremely rich and eager to contribute to their future campaign.

As already noted in this book, nothing could be further from the truth. Most of the cast and crew members make a good living, but don't qualify as wealthy. There are a handful of top actors, directors, and producers who are wealthy – but they all work extremely hard and maintain a difficult work schedule to stay on top. Dinner with a presidential candidate or the United Nations? Maybe. Dinner with a local politician? Not likely. Local politicians, then, become disillusioned when their state doesn't begin to look like Hollywood and they don't get the attention they think they deserve.

For entertainment incentives to work, the focus must be on creating jobs and building an industry. Those putting together the plan must focus on what the industry wants and needs – not on what the politicians think is best. This is true for both the incentive plan AND the regulations that define the plan. Some states have excelled at the first, but then created regulations designed to stifle the industry or drive it away entirely. Regulations that insist on the state having creative control are doomed to failure. Awarding incentives based on the subject matter, or having a committee authorized to ban scripts, are also industry-stifling plans.

The incentive plan must also be realistic about what the state can pay back to the production; several states ran into trouble by promising more incentive money than they actually could pay. Controls must be set into place to make sure that the state doesn't over-promise or over commit. Specific regulations about what "qualifies" a production must be carefully thought out. This can include types of productions (see Chapter 5 for more information), distribution deals, and end credit requirements.

Finally, local film communities must be educated to understand the value of tax credits as an incentive, not as a subsidy. Incentives bring in work opportunities from outside the state – subsidies do not. Many local filmmakers just want to make their own movies – they don't understand the industry and may have no interest in working in it. In fact, local filmmakers can actually get in their own way; they are creatives and many are not economically or politically savvy. A local film community does not (indeed, cannot) produce major motion pictures – studios are needed for that. Therefore, a state film office cannot rely on the local film community for networking, information, or productions – they must rely on studio connections. It is important to help local filmmakers understand incentives, however, because overall growth of the industry through incentives (not subsidies) creates more work for everyone and generates more opportunities for the local filmmaking community.

Once a professional workforce is developed within a state, these skilled workers must organize to educate their government about the realities of the entertainment industry. Because economic statistics can be worked in either direction (see Chapter 6), the film professionals – including ancillary vendors with equipment and props – must be visible and vocal. Local industry leaders in New Mexico and in Louisiana were very successful at lobbying their respective governors when the incentives were challenged there. It doesn't always work (for example, Florida and Michigan) but generally speaking, politicians pay attention to the louder voices.

## Partisan Politics

One of the unfortunate realities of politics today, however, is the partisan nature of it. For entertainment incentives to be effective – and continue – the plan must have bipartisan support. Jobs creation should not be relegated to just the Democrat camp or just the Republican camp.

If only one party is in favor, then a change in leadership can doom the incentive plan before it has time to grow and develop. The entertainment industry in general – and the studios in particular – watches the political landscape very closely. Any possibility of political wavering will make the decision-makers pause. They do not want to be shooting in a state when incentives are pulled; additionally, because projects are planned more than a year in advance, studios will avoid planning a production inside a state that is arguing over incentives.

Sunset dates – the end date for incentive statutes – can be both a positive and a negative. The sunset date can be perceived as a positive, since the studio knows that the incentive money will continue until that date. The sunset date inspires confidence in the state, especially when set several years in the future. The sunset date becomes a negative, however, when that date approaches and there is political wavering. Productions not qualified by the sunset date are not eligible for incentives; when faced with this situation, studio films will automatically move to another state. Florida's un-renewed sunset date drove production into nearby Georgia; virtually overnight, production fled Michigan for Ohio and other states when incentives were pulled. Michigan's losses included Marvel's *The Avengers*, which moved next door to Ohio, and *Iron Man 3*, which moved to North Carolina and eventually employed over 1,500 people as crew and extras.[1] During Florida's debate over the entertainment incentives, one lawmaker assured constituents that Hollywood "needed" the locales that only Florida could provide, and would come in spite of no incentives.[2] However, the main proponent for incentives, Florida State Senator Nancy Detert, argued that it was actually cheaper for a production to recreate Florida scenes inside Georgia and utilize the entertainment incentives than it was to shoot in Florida without incentives.[3] As she predicted, multiple television shows left Florida for Georgia or Los Angeles after the sunset date. Film production ground to a halt, with no future major productions slated for the Sunshine State.[4] As independent contractors, trained crew, and businesses relocated to Georgia, a study released by Film Florida found that the state lost more than $1.8 billion in economic impact – jobs, taxes, sales, hotels, and film-related tourism – in the three years after the state refused to re-fund the incentive program.[5]

## Corruption

Misuse of entertainment tax incentives also remains high on the watch list for state governments. Most common is the use of "kick-backs" or bribery – state officials, elected or appointed, taking money from a producer to guarantee their qualification for incentive money. But throughout the U.S., there have been numerous other examples of misusing entertainment incentives. Officials have falsified reports and used tax credits for personal purchases (even personal vehicles). Con artists have created "shell companies" to use in applying for incentives – or reported expenditures to these fake companies as being part of the "in-state" spend for qualifying. State Film Commissioners have not verified expenditures in exchange for a percentage, or have accepted estimated costs instead of receipts for actual costs. As with any enterprise involving money, if there is a way to "play" the system, someone will find a way to do it – and do it lucratively.

Regulations are the key to avoiding corruption. There must be checks and balances to the system; putting all the financial control into the hands of one or two people is a dangerous approach. The majority of the state scandals have come because one person had control of distributing all the incentive money. To avoid that possibility, financial controls must be in place. The best option is to have separate oversight: for example, an out-of-state auditor, a film commissioner who validates the film, and a financial office that distributes the incentives. An out-of-state, independent auditor is the safest way to ensure that all parties involved are above board. Someone must be assigned to verify the production company as well as the in-state companies doing business. If the incentives are contingent on expenditures going to in-state companies – as most regulations require – then there must be verification that someone within the state actually does run the company. Having a separate office actually disperse the funds or tax credits – after approval from the film office and validation from the auditor – helps keep everyone honest.

## A Final Note

Most importantly, a state and its politicians need to realize that Hollywood doesn't need them – they need Hollywood. States like Michigan and Florida learned quickly that when incentives are withdrawn, the industry goes, too. As noted, both states lost major productions and countless small businesses overnight when their governments discontinued incentives. It takes time and commitment to grow an industry and create jobs. But when used correctly, entertainment incentives can contribute to a growing economy.

When Michigan Governor Rick Snyder signed the bill ending Michigan's film incentive, he assured his constituents that "Michigan has much to offer the movie industry, including top-notch talent and beautiful backdrops that will continue to draw filmmakers to Michigan, even without taxpayer-funded incentives."[6] Where once Michigan averaged up to 30 major productions a year, since 2015 the only major productions to shoot principal photography in Michigan were the last two to receive film incentives.[7] No additional studio films or television shows have located to Michigan. Without an incentive program, Hollywood has other places to go.

## Notes

1 Eichler, A. (2011, November 16). "With Film Incentive Capped, Michigan's Movie Jobs Face an Uncertain Future." *Huffpost*. Last accessed June 24, 2017. www.huffingtonpost.com/2011/11/17/michigan-film-incentive-jobs_n_1098247.html
2 Sandberg, B. E. (2016, April 4). "Why Florida May Lose 'Ballers' and 'Bloodline' to Other State." *The Hollywood Reporter*. 422(11), 90
3 Ibid.
4 Rodriguez, R. (2017, February 5). "Miami's Film Industry is on Life Support. Can It Survive?" *Miami Herald*. Last accessed February 21, 2018. www.miamiherald.com/news/business/bizmonday/article130883349.html
5 "Florida Legislature Allows the Entertainment Industry Financial Program to Sunset,". (2016, March). *Film Florida*. Last accessed June 24, 2017. http://filmflorida.org/news/florida-legislature-allows-entertainment-industry-financial-programsunset
6 Egan, P. (2015, July 10). "Snyder Signs Bill Ending Incentives for Film Industry". *Detroit Free Press*. Last accessed June 24, 2017. www.freep.com/story/news/local/ 2015/07/10/snyder-signs-bill-ending-film-credits/29969583
7 See Michigan Film & Digital Media Office. www.michiganbusiness.org/mifilmanddigital

# 5 Infrastructure

One of the most appealing aspects about entertainment incentives is that there are little to no initial start-up costs for a state. There is no factory to build or land to donate. Because it is a mobile industry, production does not have to stay in a single location.

With that said, the industry grows best when focused around a major city and supported by a major airport. The state needs to have a focal point for the industry to grow around. Also, since most of the studios are based in Los Angeles, flights in and out must be frequent and accessible. Productions also want to be close to an airport and have an array of production support at hand in the form of ancillary companies: equipment rental, props, catering, etc. States that are committed to growing the industry can look at supporting a central location by building soundstages, building editing space, or providing a favorable climate to ancillary companies.

## Soundstages

Not all states with incentives offer soundstages, but they can be an enticing perk – especially if your state's weather doesn't always cooperate. A soundstage looks much like a large airplane hangar, although with curved edges along the floor and a lighting grid on the ceiling. It is much larger than a typical local TV studio; most soundstages can house four standard sets at a time, while a local TV studio generally houses one. Additionally, a soundstage is sound proof, and usually has a garage-door type entrance at one end, in order to offload sets.

Soundstages are used for a variety of reasons. For television shows, the primary sets can stay in place for the season, contributing to the continuity for both rehearsals and tapings. For film or television, the soundstage environment provides protection from weather delays, and creates a controllable environment. The director doesn't have to worry about planes flying overhead or people wandering into the shot. The director also has complete control over the sound and the lighting, and can create any atmosphere he or she wants. It is easier to schedule production with a soundstage; there are no permits needed or locations to scout.

For film production, a studio is an ideal place to shoot scenes that will have special effects. With the controlled environment, and the use of blue or green screens, the background will remain static while the actors move in front of it. The blue and green background is then replaced during editing and becomes a different place: a jungle, a city, or even a distant planet. This Chroma Key technology is useful for many different types of movies, but is especially utilized for superhero movies, fantasy adventures, and science fiction. These big budget productions generate a lot of spending and produce numerous jobs.

Soundstages are not necessary for a state to be successful in drawing the entertainment industry, but they can be helpful. A state with consistently good weather and varied terrain can promote those qualities in lieu of soundstages. States without those qualities can maximize their potential by adding soundstages, or finding investors who want to own soundstages, especially if the soundstages are located near a major airport.

## Editing

Available editing facilities can also be a perk for a state looking to attract the industry. In the current digital age, it is easier than ever to build cutting-edge editing suites. However, that very digital capability has also made it easier than ever to send footage electronically back to LA for editing. In other words, editing suites may be helpful for a production, but they will not be a primary draw.

On the other hand, a couple of states successfully focused *only* on post-production. Investors built editing facilities capable of handling not only film and television production, but also video-gaming and animation. Gaming turned out to be the largest draw, and provided one state with a steady stream of production. Using the editing facilities qualified them for incentive money and created consistent jobs for local residents.

## Ancillary Companies

Businesses that directly support hands-on production are one of the biggest tax bases for a local state, but are often not counted when assessing the effectiveness of incentives. These companies exist only as long as production continues flowing into the state. If incentives are discontinued, these businesses will leave the state or go bankrupt. The main ancillary companies are equipment rental, production catering, and design support.

Equipment rental is the largest and most necessary. Productions save a lot more money if they rent on location rather than rent in LA and transport the equipment to the location. Because most film productions are independent LLCs, they don't own any equipment of their own. If they are a studio production, there is some equipment available to them, but except for highly specialized equipment, it's still better to rent items on location. Besides the camera and lenses, productions rent multiple light kits and grip truck supplies, which include screens, diffusers, reflectors, umbrellas, clamps, apple boxes, extension cords, and c-stands. Additionally, equipment rentals sell expendable production supplies, such as gaffers tape, rope, light bulbs and gels that burn out or melt down during production. Equipment rental companies must hire knowledgeable people to stock their floor and assist with filling orders; this brings new, permanent jobs to the area. In general, access to equipment rental is a major component in attracting big productions to a state.

A well-fed crew is a happy, productive crew, so production catering is another vital business for the industry. When a production day begins, the cast and crew must stay on set until the day ends, anywhere from 12 to 16 hours later. Food and beverages are a necessity, then, to their well-being and productivity. Production catering is often embraced by existing catering companies, but is very different from the standard event catering. The objective on set is to provide both hot and cold options for at least two meals a day (either breakfast and lunch or lunch and "second meal") and, on big-budget films, usually hearty snacks in both the morning and afternoon. Production caterers must bring the food to the set – lots of food – and find a way to keep the hot food hot and the cold food cold, even on remote locations and even if the mealtime is delayed for an hour or more. Drinks and desserts are usually expected as well. Additionally, the food must be provided daily, something that event caterers are not always geared up for.

The cast and crew numbers will also vary from day to day; a big day with 200 background extras will certainly increase the number of people who must be fed. This can provide enormous challenges for the catering company, which has to be flexible enough to change with the production schedule yet savvy enough to shop and budget for their own food purchases. Production catering is a major undertaking, and creates multiple jobs per production; planning, shopping, cooking, delivering, serving, and clean-up are all part of the process and require many different people in order to be successful. Caterers who specialize in production meals are a necessary component in attracting the entertainment industry to a state.

The third type of ancillary support companies are usually smaller and varied, but provide design assistance to the production. These companies assist with wardrobe, props, and set construction. Support companies can provide rentals, raw materials, or even trained professionals for hire. Wardrobe, for instance, could be supported by a company that specializes in the rental of high-end fashions or period costumes. Another company may sell fabric, thread, and other items needed for the creation of costumes. A third company could provide temp work from tailors, seamstresses, fashion/style consultants, cobblers, and even milliners. Thus, three different companies could be created to help support the entertainment industry. Prop rental houses, prop makers, and prop assistants help provide the small items that are used in television and film creation. Set construction can be supported by lumber yards, hardware stores, and temp work from carpenters, electricians, and – sometimes – even plumbers. In short, these types of companies, while not required, nonetheless provide a rich environment for the entertainment company to grow and flourish.

## Conclusion

While the state government should not necessarily set up soundstages, editing facilities, or ancillary companies, it is important to provide a pro-business atmosphere that will allow these companies to exist. Many of these will fall under the heading of "small business," and, in many states, find an environment that discourages them. Excessive regulations, heavy license fees, and over-reaching bureaucracy and red-tape will stifle the existence of these companies and, ultimately, limit the growth of the entertainment industry. Financial incentives are huge, but are offset by the costs involved if the film production has to bring everything and everyone in from out of state. Protection for the small businesses that support the industry can provide big pay-offs in the long-term plan.

# 6 Making Incentives Work

The biggest obstacle for entertainment tax incentives is demonstrating their effectiveness. Unfortunately, there is no consistent measurement – not even an agreement of what *should* be measured. Because of this, both critics and supporters use the statistics to say anything they want.

## Measuring Effectiveness

A comprehensive study of state incentives in 2012 found that "inconsistent methodology" was used within states to collect data and that study results were often based on "limited data."[1] Because of these irregularities, two different groups within a state can study the effectiveness of incentives and walk away with two entirely different conclusions. One primary problem is that many times the incentives are measured by using a manufacturing model.

For many years, states have offered tax incentives to corporations to locate a factory, or manufacturing plant, within their borders. The state would offer land or a set number of tax-free years. Once the factory was built and established, it became a permanent part of the state (barring bankruptcy). Eventually the company would begin to pay taxes. Additionally, the company would provide a large number of full-time jobs, which could be easily measured; these jobs generally continued from year to year. The output of the plant could also be easily measured, in both number of items produced and in monetary value.

As Chapter 3 notes, however, this is not the way the entertainment industry works. Each production, even when backed by a studio, becomes its own LLC. Physical production can last anywhere from three weeks to six months. This makes it extremely difficult to count jobs or measure output using traditional methods. For instance, an independent camera operator may work on eight different productions within a year, at an average of six weeks per production. That adds up to 48 weeks of full-time work, with four weeks off in between productions (for vacation and holidays). In essence, the camera operator has worked a full year for a very good salary – but that work will not be measured by many economic models because it was "temporary" work for eight different companies. Yet this is how the entertainment industry works.

Occasionally, a study – or a reporter – will look at the amount of incentive money "given" to the production and divide that by the number of "full-time jobs" created with that money. Obviously, that number will show a very low return, for precisely the reasons already discussed. Another fallacy often reported by those opposed to incentives is to take the total amount of incentive money "given" to the production and divide it by the number of tax-paying households in the state. This usually reads in the papers as "this movie" cost each taxpayer "this amount," which does "nothing" but benefit "wealthy" filmmakers. Beyond the incorrect measuring (and the ignorance of the small businesses in the industry), this approach ignores the fact that productions are given tax credits as a percentage of what they *spend* in the state. In other words, the production has already spent thousands – often millions – in the state; this money is spent on things like food, space, supplies, and labor, and the state has already benefited from those expenditures. Returning 20 percent back to the production means that the state keeps 80 percent. And without the incentives, that money would have been spent in another state.

Some studies use the numbers provided by the Bureau of Labor Statistics, which does include counts on temporary employment. However, the Bureau also groups like-minded work, which can also skew the measurement of incentive effectiveness. For example, the camera operator mentioned above could be placed in the same category as the part-time teenager who takes up tickets at the local movie theater; they are both considered part of the entertainment industry by the Bureau. However, the movie theater is a separate business and is not affected by incentives in any way. It does not create a product; it is simply a distributer. Additionally, the teenager receives only the minimum wage, while the camera operator receives at least union scale. Added together, the overall "salary level" created by the "incentives" goes way down – but the teenager's job should never have been included in the first place.

Conversely, many models don't include ancillary companies or side businesses that profit from production. Existing companies receive a boost from in-state spending by productions: lumber and hardware, security companies, and hotels are all examples of businesses that profit and add to the local tax base, but are not always included when measuring the economic impact. Additionally, companies that rent out production equipment, create props or costumes, or feed hungry crew members may not be included in the measurement. Yet without the industry in state, these companies wouldn't exist; without incentives, the industry wouldn't be in the state. These companies provide jobs and pay taxes that wouldn't exist otherwise and should be counted when measuring effectiveness.

Along those lines, another common inconsistency is measuring only the productions that received incentives instead of looking at the entire production industry within a state. Not all productions apply for incentives; some don't qualify based on budget or number of shooting days. But that production may "piggy-back" off of another production, especially if attached to the same studio, by utilizing some of the same crew or similar locations. Economic models need to include all production dollars spent in the state, whether the production received incentive money or not. Ignoring some production demonstrates an ignorance of how the industry operates. Bringing in a long string of connected productions is the only way to build up the entertainment industry in a state: growing the crew base, providing a need for ancillary companies, and creating a marketing profile. Qualified productions make this happen, whether they take incentives or not.

## When Incentives Work

As discussed in Chapter 1, building out the industry within a state needs to be approached as if it were an assembly line. In order to be an effective economic engine, a state needs one production after another to enter the state. As more productions enter a state, more crew jobs are created. The higher the crew base, the more attractive the state is to the studios – and this brings in a higher level of production activity. A higher level of production activity leads to the creation of more support companies, such as equipment rentals.

### *Permanent Residents*

This creation of a local crew base and local companies contributes a lot to the local economy. These permanent residents buy homes and cars. They pay state income tax, buy local goods and services. Although this is similar for any industry, the film industry does not exist inside a state without incentive dollars. Most production jobs pay well, making the salaries closer to skilled labor or white-collar employment; in the industry, most behind-the-scenes jobs are considered "crafts."

The industry can also keep college-educated film students from fleeing the state to look for work. It costs an average of $143,000 per student to educate a child from kindergarten through high school.[2] Add in what the state supplements for higher education and the state has a sizable investment in every graduate. When a student finishes school and immediately leaves the state to work somewhere else, the state suffers a loss. The graduate is no longer an investment but a liability. While every state has at least one college-level program in media production, most states do not have enough jobs to employ those graduates. Instead, they wind up moving to states where the entertainment industry is thriving. Twenty years ago, that meant only Los Angeles or New York City. Today, graduates have many more options, with the most popular destinations being Georgia, Louisiana, and New Mexico – states that have been very successful with their tax incentive programs. Other states lose out on the potential provided by these educated students.

The highly skilled workforce also includes computer programmers and other tech employees. The entertainment industry uses computers for data wrangling, editing, animation, graphics, robotic cameras, video-gaming, and special effects, among many other areas. People who are trained on computers can learn how to make those skills count in the entertainment arena. This impact is felt the most when a state includes post-production (or editing) in their incentive package, and if the facilities are present. But data wrangling, robotic cameras, and special effects are also used *during* production, so any entertainment incentive plan can benefit.

Retraining existing labor is another way that permanent residents can be part of the film and television industry. Some states have successfully integrated training programs into their incentive package; in other states, laborers work as apprentices to Hollywood veterans in order to learn how their skills can apply to creating entertainment. One common area is carpentry. Someone skilled in building construction or woodworking can learn how those skills apply to building sets. "Sets" are the scenery for a film or television show and are usually full scale. The set can be a floor and three walls, or it can be as big as a house. Most sets have a wooden frame; many "house" sets are actually fully constructed on the outside, but a shell on the inside. The basic skills for building a set are the same as building a house, but the final product is different. People who can build houses can learn to build sets.

Sets also need other people to bring them to life. House painters and interior decorators, for example, are fully utilized by the production designer to create a realistic set. Electricians are needed to wire some sets, and may also be used to assist with setting up the lights. Sets also need realistic flooring: tile, carpet, or wood laminate must be laid down, just as in a home. People with these skill sets within a state can learn how to turn their knowledge base into an entertainment-oriented focus – and unemployed workers can find a way back onto a payroll.

Other areas of retraining include hair and make-up or costumes. People who are trained in these areas can learn how to apply those skills to actors. Hair, make-up, and costume design are all essential parts of filmmaking, but they require a specific approach due to the use of cameras and hot lights. Someone with training in hair, make-up, or costumes can apprentice with an industry professional and learn how to change over into the entertainment industry. Salaries are usually higher than in the non-entertainment sector, and this keeps these workers in state.

Keeping permanent residents – whether college students, new trainees in production, transplants, new business owners, or retrained skilled workers – can boost a state's economy. These people can command good wages in the entertainment industry, and can be good consumers of goods and services. They pay taxes, buy homes and cars, and contribute to the community. But their contributions need to be counted when measuring the effectiveness of incentives.

### *Visiting Professionals*

As mentioned previously, most studios will send industry professionals into the state for a production, at least in the short term. Sometimes they will send a large group of crew members, especially when a state is in the early stages of building up crew. This brings a need for short-term housing, either in hotels (most common) or in rental property. These expenditures are often counted for productions that receive incentives. Many times, however, these expenditures are not counted for "scouting" trips or for productions that don't receive incentives.

Scouting trips may happen before an application is submitted, so often don't qualify for incentives. The purpose of these trips is to examine the locations and make sure they are right for the film or television show. The scouting can take just a few days – or an entire month. The team can consist of just one person or as many as five. But their economic impact includes hotel, food, gas, and rental cars. Other expenditures can be made in this visit as well, including lumber and equipment rental.

### *Tourism*

According to experts, at least 5 percent of worldwide tourism is inspired directly by movies.[3] This translates into billions of dollars, especially when countries or states market the movie connection as a destination. An aggressive marketing campaign by New Zealand, the shooting location for *The Lord of the Rings* trilogy (LOTR) and *The Hobbit*, demonstrated the tremendous possibilities of film tourism. Ten years after the release of the first LOTR, a tourism official reported that 6 percent of all tourists to New Zealand cited the movies as one of the main reasons they chose to vacation there; 1 percent noted that the movies were their sole reason for visiting.[4] That one percent was worth NZD$33 million to the economy (about US$27 million).[5]

Other countries followed their lead, creating tours and destinations based on movies or television shows filmed in their area.[6] The concept has grown exponentially, leading to the travel phrase "set-jetting,"[7] or "location vacation." While U.S. states have not capitalized on the phenomenon as much as international locations have, there is still some economic boost available for those willing to market their destinations.

Film tourism, if marketed and supported, can help a state or city increase their tax base – primarily through hotel, gas, and restaurant taxes. It can also increase outside awareness of what the state has to offer productions, and can therefore recruit more projects for the local crew. Film tourism does not come organically, however; states must be aggressive about what their locations are and market to the target audience of the movie or TV show. Film tourism cannot be the primary economic engine for a state, either. It works best as an addition to an aggressive recruitment campaign from the state film office to the studios.

## When Incentives Don't Work

When entertainment incentives don't work, it can usually be traced back to one of three primary issues: overexpansion, fraud, or underperformance by the film office. Each of these scenarios can waste taxpayer money without building out the industry within a state. These are different than the use of incentives as a "political football" – in that instance, either the incentives are not given enough time to build out the industry, or politicos have used incorrect measures to determine that they don't work. This section looks at the actual reasons why some states do fail with their incentive program.

### *Overexpansion*

Offering too much, too quickly can offset the gains of an incentive program. As this book points out, growing a new industry takes time. The entertainment industry is especially slow, as it needs time to market itself, train a workforce, and attract ancillary vendors. States that offered very large percentage returns at the onset – like Michigan's 40 percent – found multiple productions in their state quickly. Unfortunately, most states don't have the crew depth necessary to meet that immediate kind of demand. In those cases, with few locals to act as crew, a state will not reap the rewards of job creation: buying houses, cars, paying property tax and income tax. They still receive expenditures from hotels, sales tax, and food. But the larger, needed benefit is job training. In Michigan's case, by the time the crew was built and ancillary companies were in place, the state government changed hands and gave up on entertainment incentives – at a point when it was just beginning to pay off. Newly trained crew found themselves without job opportunities – many relocated to Ohio or Louisiana.

Another risk of overexpansion is promising more than the state can deliver. The worst example of this is when a state approves a production for incentives, and then reneges on that promise. Sometimes the film office will argue that the production wasn't approved "in time," although that was never communicated to the producers, who worked in the state in good faith. Other times the film office will admit that the money for the tax rebates has already been spent, and there is none left for the current production – even though the production was approved and promised that money. Unfortunately, this scenario has happened frequently enough that some of the large studios require a state with caps to set the promised funds aside in a separate account until the production is shot, the audit is complete, and the incentives have been paid to the production. The cliché "once bitten, twice shy" is also extremely applicable in this case: studios do not return to states that have broken promises. Entertainment incentives are competitive enough that the studios don't need any specific state – and they have no patience for states that are unprofessional. Breaking promises will have a chilling effect on the build-out of the industry.

### *Fraud*

States that lack financial controls for their incentive program leave themselves open to fraudulent use of their money. Several states over the years have made national news when a film commissioner or politician was indicted on criminal charges ranging from bribery to financial misconduct.[8] Most of the charges stem from improper awards, such as allowing a production to count expenditures that actually do not qualify. Other film officials awarded incentives without any documentation or receipts from the production – a clear violation of their own regulations. Bribery is also a frequent topic when looking at misuse of incentives. This happens when a film office official takes money from a production for either approving a production that otherwise wouldn't qualify, moving a production to the front of the line for incentives, or for awarding incentives to a production without requiring documentation. In every case, taxpayers lose.

Filmmakers have also been brought up on charges related to wrongful use of incentive money. Beside bribery, producers have been charged with falsifying expenditure documents and receiving incentive money to which they were not entitled.[9] Others have been brought up on charges of creating shell companies within a state that were used as a pass-through company: the shell company brought in goods from outside the state, then passed them off as qualifying for in-state purchases.

Of course, fraud is not new to politics. Wherever there are large pools of money, there will be people waiting to take advantage. With film incentives, though, if there is no checks and balances in the system, the person in charge has an enormous amount of power. He or she has access to millions of dollars, making it very tempting to look the other way for a little cash under the table. A sound incentive program will ensure that there are multiple people involved in the process: at least one person to evaluate the documentation while a different person approves and disperses the final award. The power must be removed from the hands of one person.

### *Underperformance*

The state film office is the gateway to production within a state. They serve a vital role in servicing the productions that come into the state. Before incentives mushroomed, most film offices served as a type of locations office – when a production came into the state, the film office would help them find the best backgrounds to shoot in. Sometimes they would also help with local permits, but that was generally the extent of their participation. In today's competitive landscape, however, the film office must be the recruiting office for the state. Their primary job, if the state wishes to have a successful incentive program, is to develop contacts with the major studios in Hollywood. The film office must constantly network: meet with the production executives in LA who make the decisions, work the trade publications to identify upcoming productions, and educate local communities on the benefits production can bring.

Once a production has been recruited, the film office must work to meet the needs of that production. Studio executives have high expectations for a film office. Most importantly, they want to know that someone in the film office will be available 24/7 to assist if the production runs into a snag. The studio may also ask for assistance in securing permits, recruiting local crew and extras, and/or networking with local communities. The studio also expects a quick turnaround on both the incentive application and on the incentive award. For Hollywood, time is money, and patience is not a virtue possessed by many.

Because of these expectations, the head of the film office should be someone with extensive production experience. Having someone who can identify with the process, who understands the demands of production, provides an extra layer of confidence to the studio executives. It is even better if this person has worked in the Hollywood system and has connections; those connections are invaluable when establishing a recruiting plan. The entertainment industry is relationship driven. Unfortunately, too many states look at the head of the film office as a political appointment. Political appointees with no production experience and no industry connections make poor, ineffective leaders. Their film offices often wind up as phone operators: they assist any productions that call, but do little to nothing in recruiting. This leads to a state with sporadic production that generates few local crew jobs. Any state without an assembly line of productions constantly moving into the state will not grow out the industry and will not see a positive return on their incentive investment. A lazy or uninformed film office is a severe detriment to a state, regardless of how good the incentive package is.

## Making Incentives Work

A successful film incentive package will grow out the entertainment industry within a state, adding jobs and contributing to the tax base. Making that incentive plan successful, however, takes multiple steps that are all important to the process. Here is that checklist:

- The film office must be run by a production professional
- The incentive plan must be valuable to the industry, but realistic for the state
- The regulations must match the legislation *and* the realities of the industry
- There must be checks and balances in place to avoid fraud
- The application process must match the legislation, and have a quick turnaround process
- The incentives should focus on productions that will build out the industry[10]
- There must be specific measurements established at the beginning of the incentive program; these must be adhered to and communicated to the state. These include:
    - Jobs created, including temporary and part-time
    - Crew database, especially the growth of the database over time
    - New businesses started that are related to the entertainment industry
    - Infrastructure additions
    - Total amount *spent* by productions in the state (and must include *all* productions, not just those receiving incentive money)
- The film office must network constantly with the studios, and must implement an aggressive marketing plan to recruit productions
- The film office must meet the needs of productions that come into the state, especially studio-backed productions
- The film office must constantly market the benefits of the incentive program to the public, the media, and to elected officials.

States must also realize that this is not an overnight process. Building out this industry takes time, but has economic benefits if given the time to grow. Georgia is an excellent example of what a focused, well-run incentives program can do for a state. For fiscal year 2016, productions spent $2.02 billion in the state, generating an economic impact of $7.2 *billion*.[11] Of that, $4.2 billion was in wages alone. Georgia set up a solid incentive program, grew the crew base, added infrastructure such as studios, and aggressively marketed the state to both television and film productions. They have recently earmarked some of the proceeds from the incentive program to fund a training program for crew members, ensuring that the state continues its successful path. Georgia is now third in the nation for total production dollars spent in the state, behind only California and New York.[12] In 2016, however, Georgia was number 1 for total number of top 100 feature films.[13] With a booming industry, job growth, and economic development, Georgia demonstrates what a successful incentive program looks like.

## Notes

1 Kulesza, M., Crespi, C. S., and Mihalek, P. (2012). "Examining Incentive-Based State Tax Legislation in the Film Industry". *Journal of Applied Financial Research*, 2, 57.
2 U.S. Census Bureau 2014 Annual Survey of School System Finances, reported in August 2016; most recent data available. Accessed March 2, 2017. www.census.gov/library/publications/2016/econ/g14-aspef.html
3 Cha, F. (2013, February 22). "Hollywood: World's Most Dramatic Travel Agent?". *CNN*. Last accessed July 1, 2017. http://travel.cnn.com/lights-cameracountry-power-and-glamour-film-tourism-735306
4 Pinchefsky, C. (2012, December 14). "The Impact (Economic and Otherwise) of *Lord of the Rings/The Hobbit* on New Zealand." *Forbes*. Last accessed July 3, 2017. www.forbes.com/sites/carolpinchefsky/2012/12/14/the-impact-economicand-otherwise-of-lord-of-the-ringsthe-hobbit-on-new-zealand/#2885ab6031b6
5 Ibid.
6 For an in-depth analysis, see Sue Beeton, *Film-Induced Tourism*. N.p. Clevedon, UK; Buffalo, NY: Channel View Publications, 2005.
7 Attributed to *New York Post* travel reporter Gretchen Kelly, February 19, 2008.
8 Verrier, R. (2011, January 19). "Iowa Film Tax Credit Program Racked by Scandal." *Los Angeles Times*. Last accessed July 5, 2017. http://articles.latimes.com/2011/jan/19/business/la-fi-ct-onlocation-20110119
9 McNary, D. (2011, January 19). "Peter Hoffman Convicted on Tax Credit Fraud in Louisiana." *Variety*. Last accessed July 5, 2017. http://variety.com/2015/film/news/peter-hoffman-convicted-on-tax-credit-fraud-in-louisiana-1201480899/. *Also see* Robert Wood. (2012, June 5) "Beware Film and Other Tax Shelter Deals That Go Criminal." *Forbes*. Accessed July 5, 2017. www.forbes.com/sites/robertwood/2012/06/05/beware-film-and-other-tax-shelter-deals-that-go-criminal/#7e4dcb1014b8

10 See Chapter 7 for a full discussion on which productions will build out the industry, and which do not.

11 Lynch, J. (2017, April 9). "Georgia's TV and Film Industry Now Brings in $7 Billion a Year, Fueled by Smart Incentives." *Adweek*. Last accessed July 7, 2017. www.adweek.com/tv-video/how-atlanta-became-the-worlds-fastestgrowing-film-and-tv-destination

12 Ibid.

13 "Fourth Annual Feature Film Study." (May 23, 2017). *Film LA*. Last accessed July 7, 2017. www.filmla.com/filml-a-issues-fourth-annual-feature-film-study-california-in-fourth-place-among-international-competitors-for-feature-film-projects/

# 7 Avoiding Pitfalls

As discussed in previous chapters, for entertainment tax incentives to be successful there must be an on-going string of productions. This builds up the workforce, as well as the ancillary companies that support the industry. Unfortunately, many states use their incentive funds to support productions that don't create jobs. Using incentive money to fund productions that can't deliver also reduces the prospect of luring the high-profile productions that *can* deliver. All states have a limit to the amount of incentives that can be offered, so it just makes sense to put that money toward productions that will contribute to economic growth. This chapter will discuss which productions to court and which to avoid.

## Successful Types of Production

Scripted television does more to grow the industry than any other medium. While filmmaking is seen as more high profile, a single production usually lasts only a few months at most. A successful television drama or comedy series usually shoots for eight to ten months each year, and therefore creates steady jobs for a longer period of time. Once a TV series settles into a state, its production will usually stay as long as the series airs. There have been exceptions, especially when a state removes incentives, but most productions don't want the expense of moving sets or rebuilding sets. If the incentives stay in place, the production will usually stay.

A scripted series usually hires many local people, especially in the trade or skills area. Additionally, crew brought in from Los Angeles will either move to the new state, buying or renting a home and adding to the local tax base, or will train locals to replace them when they return to LA. A well-crafted incentive program will include a trainee program so that locals will ultimately replace the majority of out-of-state crew. Both approaches provide revenue that will be spent in the state and add to income tax, sales taxes, property taxes, and gasoline taxes. A television series is also in a better position to hire recent college graduates as production assistants (PAs), which provides an entry-level job into multiple areas of production. Internships are easier for a television series to provide as well, since they will be in production for eight to ten months out of the year. All in all, a scripted television series production will provide more jobs overall and will do more to build out the industry in a state than any other production.

A television series always starts with a pilot. A pilot is one completed episode, the first in what is hoped to be a series. It is basically a "test" episode, or prototype, used to sell the show to advertisers and the networks. For incentives, most states have separate applications for "series" versus "pilot," understanding that a pilot budget (one show) has a larger budget than the "episodics" (multiple installments) that will follow. The average cost of a half-hour comedy pilot for a network is around $2 million; the average cost of a one-hour network drama pilot runs around $5–$6 million. In contrast, the average cost of the weekly network episode is around $100,000 up to $250,000; 13 episodes is the norm for a series. Because of the higher budget for pilots, some states have made network television pilots a primary focus. This creates numerous jobs during the network "pilot season" each year, which runs from January through March, with post-production (editing) taking place in March and April. Additionally, pilots are also shot more like films; they have more shooting days than the weekly episodes and usually hire more crew.

There is another benefit to recruiting pilots: if a pilot is shot within a state, and the pilot is picked up for a cable or network schedule, the production will usually return to that same location for the series. This gives that state a television series and a better shot at building out the industry. The downside: not every pilot gets picked up, so it's always a gamble. In fact, for fall 2017, out of 450 pilots created, only 74 were picked up by the networks.[1] Once picked up, there is no guarantee that the series will last. If it lasts the full season, it has a good chance of being picked up for the next year, but cancellation is always a looming possibility. Sometimes a cable network will pick up the series and continue it. One other positive is the emergence of streaming services such as Hulu and Netflix. In addition to creating their own content, they have given new life to programs cancelled by the networks.

### *Filmmaking*

The oldest production medium, filmmaking dates back to 1878. Although the process has changed dramatically over the years with advancements in technology, the basic storytelling concept has remained. Film production, while based in Los Angeles, has always taken place in many countries around the world. In the 1950s, entertainment industry professionals coined the term "runaway production," initially used to describe any film shot outside of the U.S. After the growth of state incentives, however, "runaway production" grew to include any film or television show shot outside of California. There are two general types of runaways: "creative runaways" and "economic runaways." "Creative runaways" exist when a distant location is selected for the specific physical background needed to tell the story, i.e., going to Paris to shoot a movie about the Eiffel Tower. In today's landscape, however, technology can replicate any place on earth – or beyond. Instead of being "creative runaways," then, many productions locate to places where the incentives are best and can support their budget. These are called "economic runaways," and are often driven by a decision by the studio in consultation with the producer and/or director.

This is a positive for states who want to build out the entertainment industry. Although the landscape/location (mountains, ocean, etc.) is part of the decision, it is no longer the *main* part of the decision. A state can do a very credible job of building out the industry by attracting one project after another through the use of incentives and experienced crew. As noted previously, however, the "assembly line" concept must be in place to ensure economic development and make a solid case for the incentives to exist. There is an economic impact if that assembly line is stopped. It is imperative, then, for the film office to be constantly courting the studios and major producers; this ensures that when one production "wraps," another production begins – and jobs continue. Recruiting is now the core job of a state film office, not recommending locations as in the distant past.

In choosing film projects to bring to the state, the two biggest considerations are production budget and studio backing. A big-budget studio film, for example, will spend more, hire more locals, and generate more marketing bang for the state's incentive buck. A moderate budget with studio backing will also benefit the state, albeit in a smaller way. Moderate budgets don't spend as much or hire as many people, but the studio backing means that the film will probably be seen in theaters – and this will generate more interest in the state for future projects. Additionally, a studio may "test-drive" a state with a small or moderate budget film or television production; if the production goes well and the state is rated as a success, the studio will send bigger pictures that way. Keep in mind that the industry decision-makers are a small pool – and they talk to each other.

Many states wind up having to start with smaller, independent films. In those situations, look for films that already have a distribution deal in place, even if it's not with a major studio. The distribution deal means that it will probably be seen in theaters. Before spending those incentive dollars, research the pedigree. Look on the application for a producer or director who has been successful, or for an actor who is established. Several "Best Picture" nominees at the Oscars in 2017 (for films made in 2016) were independent films – but each one had a distribution deal and at least one "name" in their production or on the producing/distribution team. Films without a distribution deal often end up being seen only at film festivals. While this supports the arts, it does not help a state build out the industry.

Films to avoid are the low-budget, independent films with no distribution deal and no union connections. These films often look for volunteer cast and crew; they provide very few, if any, local paid positions. The film may not even make it into a significant film festival, meaning that very few people will ever see it. If the producers have no connections, then it will not generate future productions for the state. In short, providing incentive money for this type of production is a waste of taxpayer dollars. They don't create jobs, provide marketing credentials, or establish industry connections. States that provide money only to this type of production will not be successful in building out the entertainment industry in their area.

## Other Productions to Avoid

Many states have broadened their incentive dollars to include other types of productions, often with bad results. One of the most common problem areas is with unscripted television, usually called "reality" television. A number of these shows have a distribution deal or network affiliation, and many are very popular, so they seem like a good investment for the state. The problem is that most of them use a very small crew, and rarely hire more than one or two people within a state. They build fewer sets, and shoot a shorter number of days. This means that they spend less than a scripted series and don't generate jobs. In the industry, they are considered a niche group; supporting reality television, then, rarely leads to attracting episodic television (where the real money is). Additionally, many of the reality shows have given a "black-eye" to the states where they are shot, because viewers believe everyone in the state acts like the people in the show. It simply doesn't help a state that is trying to lure million-dollar productions.

Other productions that are a bad investment for a state include music videos and commercials. Music videos seem like a good investment because they often have a music "name" attached. From a production standpoint, however, they don't help a state build out the entertainment industry. First, music video crews are even smaller than reality television crews. Most of the time, the entire crew comes in from another state, which doesn't generate local jobs. The in-state spend for a music video is also relatively small; although they will use hotel rooms and restaurants, the shooting days will usually be minimal. Many music videos are shot in a two-day period. They require few, if any, sets and make very few purchases in state. Last, the music industry doesn't have much overlap with the film and television industry; connections made with one don't equate to connections with the other. Any incentive money spent on music videos will generate only more music video opportunities: no new jobs, little local revenue, and few new connections.

Commercials are largely the same as music videos: small crew, few local hires, and no connections to film or television production. While most states require a group of commercials within a certain budget, this still doesn't lead to new jobs. Again, physical production usually only lasts a few days and most of the crew will come in from out of state. There are no screen credits attached to a commercial, either, so marketing is limited for the state. Generally speaking, then, providing incentive money for commercials doesn't pay off in terms of jobs, revenue, or recruiting.

## Conclusion

Scripted television and studio-backed films are the safest way for a state to build out the entertainment industry. These productions create more local jobs and support more local businesses than any other production. Independent films can be a great way to start the process, as long as the film has a solid pedigree and a distribution deal. Other types of productions – such as films with no distribution deal, reality television, music videos, and commercials – have proven to be less successful, and even a drain on an incentive program.

States looking to be successful need three things: production professionals in the film office, a solid application process, and a plan to market the state to Hollywood. The application needs to identify the people associated with the production – including actors and producers – as well as the distribution plan and any studio connection. The budget needs to be considered, as well as any unions affiliated with the production. In this way, film offices can make sure that the incentive money will be used to hire local people and recruit future projects.

For the marketing plan, a successful state will reach out to the studios, large and small, and demonstrate a desire to work with them. Attending the annual "Location Managers" fair in Los Angeles each year doesn't count. Location managers rarely select the state where the production will be shot; instead, they find the best locations within the selected state. Actually choosing the state is decided at the studio or producing level. A state that neglects the studio system will not be successful in the long run. Additionally, a film office that merely sits back and waits for phone calls from productions will wind up dealing with only the productions that other states don't want. This approach will not build out the entertainment industry and will waste taxpayer dollars.

Most importantly, the film office personnel must have an extensive background in production and a complete understanding of how the industry works. They need to be knowledgeable about the needs of a large studio production and yet understanding about the limitations of a smaller, independent film. The film office must have connections to facilitate networking and be available 24/7 to solve problems whenever a large studio production is in the state. In short, the personnel of the film office become the face of the state to the entire industry. They are critical to the success of the incentives.

## Note

1 Goldberg, L. (2017, February 13). "TV Pilot Season 2017: By the Numbers". *The Hollywood Reporter*. Last accessed February 1, 2018. www.hollywoodreporter.com/live-feed/tv-pilot-season-2017-by-numbers-975350

# 8 The Union Equation

Since the majority of actors and crew members in the entertainment industry are independent contractors, unions and guilds are an integral part of the industry. Technically, both guilds and unions are collective bargaining organizations. The primary difference is that unions typically represent employees while guilds represent independent contractors. Both guilds and unions are represented in the entertainment industry; "guild" is usually the preferred terminology among industry insiders, but "union" is more familiar to those outside the industry. Both words are also often used interchangeably, even among those who know the difference. In this chapter, then, union will refer to both guilds and unions.

In either case, the entertainment industry guilds and unions are extremely important because they provide health coverage, pensions, and many other benefits that would otherwise be out of reach for the self-employed. While some of the most successful incentive states are formally "right-to-work" states, unions are still a big part of the equation. Part of this is because of the benefits to the individual, but the biggest reason is the connection to the studios. Because Hollywood is a union town, all of the studios participate only in union, or signatory, productions.

Many independent productions also participate as signatory productions in spite of their smaller budgets. This is because distribution is very difficult if your production is not union specific; studios and networks can't work with you if you are non-union. Even student films sign agreements with the unions, especially the Screen Actors Guild – it's the only way to get professional actors with any experience. The unions, in turn, have provided lower rates for productions with lower budgets, including a student-friendly option. This has strengthened the use of unions in the entertainment industry, even as union popularity in general has decreased in the U.S.[1]

Union rates work on two levels. First, unions set the pay scale for the actors and crew on a production. Called "union scale," this varies from low to high based on the budget for the production, but provides a base guarantee for the laborer. Second, unions and guilds also charge the production a fee for the use of experienced, skilled labor. Listed under "fringes" in the budget (fringes may also include federal tax and FICA, etc.), the union sets a percentage contribution made back to the union for each union member who works on the production.

The unions and guilds also provide standards and support for their members during production. Since days on a set can be really long (often 12 hours), the unions set guidelines for breaks, meals, length of work day, overtime pay, and meal penalties. There is a lot of flexibility on these issues, so unions/guilds negotiate these items with each individual production on behalf of their members. This negotiation process can be lengthy – and involves multiple unions and guilds – but reduces surprise financial charges for the production. The process also provides better communication between the production and the union members, since both sides know what to expect. The negotiations are usually a collaborative effort, aiming for the best guidelines for both the people and the production.

One of the primary benefits of working with a studio is union support. Each studio has designated people (or sometimes even a department) whose sole job is to build bridges with the guilds and unions – both in California and in any other states where production is based. Because of their connections, they are able to negotiate well with local divisions. These studio representatives stay up to date on the leadership, membership, and expectations of the unions, and try to create a win-win scenario in negotiations. They also represent numerous studio productions, which gives them a kind of "bulk-rate" advantage. With some groups, such as SAG-AFTRA, they may already have a collective bargaining agreement in place. Independent producers without studio backing, however, must negotiate with the unions on their own.

According to the California Film Commission, there are at least 16 guilds or unions for the industry.[2] This chapter will focus on the four organizations that have the most impact on production outside of LA: SAG-AFTRA, IATSE, DGA, and the Teamsters.

## SAG-AFTRA

The Screen Actors Guild and the American Federation of Television and Radio Artists (SAG-AFTRA) represents more than 160,000 performers.[3] Originally two separate guilds, SAG and AFTRA merged in 2012 following a vote of their membership. Commonly referred to as SAG, this guild represents actors, broadcast journalists, video game actors, dancers, recording artists, and many other types of performers. SAG-AFTRA is based in Los Angeles, but has offices in more than 20 different cities across the U.S. – including every major production hub. The guild is a member of the AFL-CIO.

For the entertainment industry, SAG-AFTRA's focus is on the actors. This includes major stars, character actors, extras, children, and even animal actors. For these performing artists, SAG-AFTRA negotiates wages and working conditions. For child actors (anyone under age 18), the guild provides additional support through the Young Performers Committee. This committee lobbies on behalf of child actors, offers tools and advice for both child actors and their parents, and provides individual state requirements for productions that utilize child actors.

For animal actors, SAG-AFTRA maintains an in-depth database for their care and protection while on set. Animal actors include any living species that is not human or plant. Besides mammals, this includes all insects, reptiles, arachnids, birds, and fish. Guidelines include set temperature, housing while in production, feeding, and other, species-specific requirements. SAG-AFTRA requires productions using live animals to register with the American Humane Association, which will monitor on-set conditions for the animal during the entire production; if the AHA is satisfied, it will award its "No Animals Were Harmed" end credit.

SAG-AFTRA comes into play on the majority of U.S. productions, because professional actors are used in most productions. This includes animation and gaming because of the voice-over work involved. In years past, SAG actors would occasionally work for a non–signatory production under the table, sometimes as a favor to a friend. Now SAG-AFTRA offers varied rates, including scale for low-budget, independent movies, and even scale rates for student films. This has increased the power of the guild; even undergraduate students can sign up with SAG-AFTRA and use professional actors. While more and more independent films are being made, fewer and fewer use non-SAG talent. Additionally, a low-budget or student film can sign up with SAG-AFTRA without signing up with another union. However, it is technically still considered a non-union picture if the production signs with SAG-AFTRA but does not sign up with IATSE and the Teamsters.

## IATSE

The International Alliance of Theatrical Stage Employees, Moving Picture Technicians, Artists and Allied Crafts of the United States, Its Territories and Canada (IATSE) represents more than 130,000 behind-the-scenes workers.[4] Branding itself as "The Union Behind Entertainment," IATSE has 375 local chapters in the U.S. and Canada – including at least one in every state.[5] The "Motion Picture & TV Production Department" of IATSE is made up of the skilled craftspeople who operate below-the-line on productions. These skills include designing and building sets, cinematography, sound, costume design, make-up, hair, gaffers, grips, electricians, lighting, props, and editing – and many more. IATSE is a member of the AFL-CIO.

IATSE negotiates wages, work hours, benefits, and safe conditions for its members. The union also provides educational opportunities and workshops to help members stay up to date on the skills and technologies in the production field. IATSE organizes general safety workshops on Occupational Safety and Health Administration (OSHA) guidelines, offers health benefits, and handles grievance procedures. Because of the growth of tax incentives, IATSE implemented an "Area Standards Agreement." This agreement allows productions outside of Los Angeles and New York City to offer lower wages for IATSE crew members. This change helped make productions in other states even more financially appealing to producers and aided in growing IATSE locals across the U.S. and Canada.

In fact, IATSE local chapters in Georgia and Louisiana are now among the largest chapters in the country, in spite of the fact that these two states are "right-to-work" states. Between 2003 and 2014, Georgia's IATSE membership grew by more than 1,000 percent, making it the largest IATSE center outside of Los Angeles and New York.[6] Louisiana has seen a membership increase of 900 percent during this same time period.[7]

IATSE is a major player in the production world. This union represents the skilled labor needed to make a film or television production work. From design to implementation, IATSE makes sure that its members are trained, knowledgeable, and up to date. Studio productions will not operate without skilled IATSE members, and many independent filmmakers also depend on them for their skill and experience. The difference, of course, is in the cost. Union productions have set wages that are much higher than negotiated wages with non-union. However, experienced union crew members are often faster and more efficient at their jobs; some producers find that this skill set offsets the higher salary costs. Occasionally, a production will find union members willing to work on a non-union production if work opportunities are lean. If the local IATSE chapter finds out, though, they will usually picket the production until it either goes signatory or drops the union crew.

## The DGA

The Directors Guild of America (DGA) protects the "creative and economic rights" of the directing team; it currently has 16,000 members.[8] Based in Hollywood, this craft labor union represents directors, assistant directors, unit production managers, associate directors, production associates, and stage managers. All of the major studios are signatories to the DGA and cannot hire directors who are not members. The DGA does offer low-budget options for independent films, which are flexible enough that most productions can use a DGA-member team. While the DGA has only a few satellite offices, they have field representatives who can assist with contract negotiations or disputes.

Economically, the DGA provides rate cards for signatory productions and also sets standards for residual payments – income provided to DGA directors on the profits made after distribution. The DGA also offers health plans and a pension fund for its members.

Creatively, the DGA protects the director in several ways. It guarantees that the director is creatively involved in all aspects of filmmaking, and that only one person can be named as director on a film. The director has other specified rights, including selection of the First Assistant Director, casting selection, and direction of any needed re-shoots. The director is also assured of a first "director's cut" during editing.

While the DGA has a smaller in-state footprint than IATSE or SAG-AFTRA, it still plays an important role in production. Locations within a state are decided by the directorial team, and the team also has a direct conduit back to the producer and to the studio. How the DGA team feels about their experience in a state has a big impact on future productions.

## The Teamsters

While not an entertainment union per se, the International Brotherhood of Teamsters is a necessary part of every union production. Branded as "North America's Strongest Union," the Teamsters are also America's biggest union with 1.4 million members in 1,900 affiliated locals.[9] The structure of the Teamsters puts a lot of the decision-making power back into these locals. With 23 different divisions, the Teamsters represent a diverse range of laborers: freight drivers, passenger drivers, airline workers, rail workers, dairy, construction, breweries, convention and trade shows, and many others. The entertainment industry is represented by the "Motion Picture & Theatrical Trade Division," which has 18 different locals across the U.S.[10]

For productions, Teamsters operate as drivers. Their biggest responsibility is hauling the equipment and set pieces from one location to another, often in large trucks. They drive passenger vans of crew members to locations and sometimes even drive vehicles in front of the camera. Teamsters can also drive heavy equipment if needed for a production.

Since not all Teamster locals have a production-specific division, going into other states can mean explaining the needs of a production to a local Teamster group. This is where studio representatives can be most helpful. They not only have experience in working and negotiating with Teamsters all across the U.S.; they also have connections and networking opportunities. Independent producers can find these negotiations to be more challenging, since the Teamsters are not a traditional entertainment union.

## Conclusion

Unions and guilds are a powerful force in the entertainment industry, whether the state is a "right-to-work" state or not. Their purpose is not to stand in the way of production or a state's incentive plan; it is quite the opposite. These unions and guilds set a collaborative tone for the industry, and can become a valuable ally for a state and its incentive plan. Since the distribution of television and movies is headquartered in Los Angeles, most of the studios have standing agreements with these organizations – especially SAG-AFTRA, the DGA, and IATSE. States that want to succeed with incentives, and create a local economic force, need to understand the power and purpose of these groups. States need to embrace the potential, and work with these unions in order to build out a strong, growing industry.

## Notes


1 Ng, D. (2017, May 9). "Hollywood Guilds Flex Their Muscle as Union Influence Declines Nationwide." *The Los Angeles Times*. Last accessed July 10, 2017. www.latimes.com/business/ hollywood/la-fi-ct-hollywood-unions-20170509-story.html

2 "California Film Commission. Production Resources: Guilds & Unions." Accessed July 16, 2017. http://film.ca.gov/production/associations-guilds/

3 "SAG-AFTRA – About Us." Accessed July 14, 2017. www.sagaftra.org/content/about-us

4 "IATSE – About Us." Accessed July 26, 2017. www.iatse.net/about-iatse

5 Ibid.

6 Robb, D. (2014, May 21). "Where Hollywood's Union Jobs Are Going: Call These States 'The Runaway 3,'" *Deadline.com*. Accessed July 28, 2017. http://deadline.com/2014/05/hollywood-runaway-production-tax-credits-georgia-louisiana-iatse-733335

7 Ibid.

8 "History of the DGA." Accessed February 5, 2018. www.dga.org/The-Guild/History.aspx

9 "Teamsters history." Accessed February 5, 2018. https://teamster.org/about/who-are-teamsters

10 "Division: Motion Picture & Theatrical Trade, State: All Locals." Accessed February 5, 2018. https://teamster.org/locals/391/All

# 9 Benefit Businesses

Ancillary companies, or vendors, as discussed in Chapter 4, are businesses that exist only when the entertainment industry is present. Benefit businesses, on the other hand, already exist within a state, but receive an additional economic impact when production is present. While businesses such as hotels and restaurants certainly benefit, there are other businesses that are less obvious. This chapter looks briefly at a few specific types of businesses that benefit in major ways, yet are generally overlooked and unrecognized as being part of the industry. While not intended to be a complete list, a focus on white-collar businesses – banking, security, insurance, and law – shows that they can all receive additional boosts from production. However, these companies are rarely considered when measuring the effectiveness of incentives; indeed, it would be very difficult to measure the specific success garnered by the entertainment industry as opposed to other industries. But the economic impact is real and should be recognized.

## Banking

Local banks can benefit in numerous ways. Since even a small production can run into several million dollars – and a major production can run upward of $100 million – the banking industry can find multiple ways to profit through lending or managing. One of the biggest is by working with investors to secure financing for a motion picture or television show. There are many different ways this can be done, but here are three examples.

### *Pre-Sales*

Some banks offer production loans or lines of credit based on pre-sales agreements and contracts executed between the producer and the distributor. The amount of capital loaned by the bank is determined by certain criteria, such as the talent and crew attached to the film, sales projections, and the marketing approach. Most of these types of investments require loaned capital to be paid back to the bank prior to the producer profiting. Generally a completion bond company is put in place to ensure the production is finished and ready for distribution in a timely manner.

### *Negative Pickup*

In a negative pickup, a producer has a signed agreement with a studio or distributor that they will purchase his/her completed film at a specific time for a specific price. Until then, the financing is up to the producer, who must pay any additional costs if the film goes over-budget. Banks feel comfortable lending the value of the contract since the guarantee is in place to pay back the loan with interest, or they may take an origination fee. Some refer to this as "factoring paper." Again, a completion bond company is hired to make sure the production is completed in a timely manner.

### *Incentives*

To receive incentives, a production only receives the tax credits *after* the production is complete and all production expenditures are filed. If a producer finds they need more money for a project than the initial investment covers, gap financing from a bank is secured to cover the production expenditures. These gap loans are less risky, because the bank knows that the loan can be repaid once the tax credits are issued (and, usually, sold or transferred). In this case, the bank profits from the interest and fees on the gap loans.

### *Other Banking Areas*

Finance is not the only way the banking industry profits from production, however. Payroll and general expenditures for production must go through a bank. Because each production is a separate LLC, there is not a designated "company bank" that is used every time. Instead, the producers can select something national, something convenient, or just a company that makes it worth their while. Again, productions spend millions and millions of dollars when cameras are rolling; with a few exceptions, the majority of the budget is spent during the production phase. Payroll is the biggest expenditure, especially for a large production. Between crew members and extras, there can be hundreds of people paid each week. There are also production payments for housing, food, transportation, and equipment rentals. Factor in the pre-production – building sets, sewing costumes, scouting – and the costs rise even higher. These expenditures involve banking at every level.

## Security

Security companies, off-duty police officers, and military veterans get a big boost from entertainment production. Security concerns have expanded in recent years, driving up the need for more people in this area. Security personnel are needed during the day to watch over cast, crew, and equipment; they also provide crowd control and manage traffic. At night, guards make sure the equipment is secure and protected. And for larger productions, security guards also maintain the secrecy required for protecting the story. This means keeping tourists and fans away from the sets, collecting any script pages that inadvertently get loose, and prohibiting unauthorized filming or pictures.

Technology has greatly increased the need for more security. Social media, drones, smaller cameras, and other advancements have made it much more difficult to protect both people and intellectual property. Social media provides a platform that drives fandom; users can post about fan sightings, upload "selfies" with their favorite star, and post other pictures from the set – almost always unauthorized. Smaller cameras, especially phone cameras, have made it much more difficult to control these photos while shooting on location. Drones can now sneak in to closed sets to take pictures. And in addition to the posting platform, social media also provides detailed information about where movies are being shot and who is on the set, driving other fans to that location. Leaked scripts also make their way online, along with fan opinions about whether the film will be good or not. Controlling all of these variables now requires more security than ever, just to protect the integrity of the film.

Entertainment security is considered a specialty area in the security business, but is easily translated from regular security. The difference is in the hours, locations, and specific requirements. Because productions maintain long hours, security is usually contracted for 24 hours a day, seven days a week. While a factory or warehouse may need only one or two guards at night, a production set may need six or more. On-set security is also a very active profession, not one of sitting and watching monitors. Security guards need to be trained in multiple areas: to watch for fire, manage traffic, manage crowds, and even guard celebrities. Security rarely happens in just one place, either; security companies must move with the sets and locations – and sometimes must guard more than one location in any given day. And when a production travels from one location to another, the security company is responsible for the protection of people and equipment during the move.

In short, states that build out the industry will see an increase in the need for security companies. Existing security companies that embrace this specialty will find a great benefit in doing so. This will increase the number of people employed, adding to the economy of the state. Again, however, these jobs – and their economic impact – are rarely counted in measuring the impact of film tax incentives.

## Insurance

Film production insurance is a foundation of the industry. It protects the studio, the producers, the crew, the equipment, the locations, and even the project itself. Considered a specialty area in the insurance industry, local insurance companies within a state can add this area on. Their brokers or agents can receive training and become a licensed production insurance broker.

The producer carries the major responsibility of acquiring insurance for a production; experts agree that the cost begins at 2.5 percent of the production budget, but can go higher depending on the needs of the production. For a small budget movie of $12 million, that means that more than $300,000 would be spent on insurance. For a movie with a big budget, however – $150 million – the insurance needs would start at more than $3 million. Insurance is a necessary big-ticket item.

For television, the production company will often purchase an annual policy. For film LLCs, however, the insurance will usually be on a short-term, per project basis. The policies usually cover liability from injuries or accidents on set, loss and theft, and libel. The size of the policy will vary depending on the other factors: total number of people, amount and type of equipment, travel involved, vehicles used, and locations selected. Other factors will drive the cost of the policy up; use of pyro, weapons, animals, aircraft, water, or underwater equipment will all significantly increase the cost. In addition to production policies, many independent contractors in the production industry will purchase their own workers' comp packages through their individual LLC.

This makes entertainment insurance a big business. Some states allow insurance expenditures to count toward qualifying expenditures (for incentives) only if they are purchased in that state. The insurance industry grows, therefore, whenever the entertainment industry is built in a state. Additionally, as people move in from other states – or people find new jobs in the industry – regular insurance needs grow as well. Life, home, and auto policies add to the bottom line for both the insurance industry and the local economy.

## Attorneys

The law profession cuts a wide swath through the entertainment industry. Entertainment law encompasses a tremendous array of topics: intellectual property, contracts, labor, clearances, taxation, business, and litigation, just to name a few. The bulk of entertainment law is practiced in California and New York; because of the studio system, most of the large contracts are handled in these states. However, many smaller legal issues are handled locally within states that house the entertainment industry.

One of the most common local needs for an attorney is setting up LLCs for independent contractors. As noted in Chapter 3, most cast and crew members in the entertainment industry operate as independent contractors, hired for each individual production. As the industry grows locally, and more crew members are trained, the need for assistance in creating LLCs grows. For cast members, most of the celebrity talent uses attorneys in California; however, as locals become extras and character players, they also find a need to incorporate for tax purposes.

There is also a great deal of basic business to be done for productions and individual LLCs. Basic business paperwork, talent releases, labor agreements, and clearances are all a big part of entertainment law. It is known, especially at local levels, to be very document-intense. Additionally, as the entertainment industry grows within a state, more writers and creators look for protection for their intellectual property.

Working as an entertainment attorney requires a law degree, but not a specific law specialty. Instead, a lawyer wanting to move into this area should focus on understanding the industry and building bridges to producers, cast, and crew. Also, to be successful, it is imperative to understand the specific regulations imposed by California law and New York law, since these will impact local productions as well.

## Other Areas

There are numerous other professions that benefit from increased production within a state. Besides restaurants and hotels – which are usually included in incentive considerations – other existing professions are needed and utilized by entertainment productions. Accountants are needed by productions, especially for payroll, but are also needed by the state to serve as independent auditors. Airline companies will boost activity and revenue when the industry is built within a state. Actors and producers are "frequent fliers" and studio executives will also fly into the state both before and during production. Rental car companies will receive additional activity as well; a small production will rent an average of three vans or large transport vehicles. A large production will rent ten or more vehicles, just to transport cast and crew. Productions also need "picture cars," the cars and pickup trucks that appear in front of the camera and are often rented by the week. Finally, companies that haul freight – whether by air, truck, rail, or water – will find additional work when productions are established within a state. Each of these professions, then, will add to their own bottom line as well as contribute to the revenue of a state. These added jobs and increased revenue benefit everyone.

## Conclusion

Many white-collar professions benefit from the growth of the entertainment industry within a state. Some of the most impacted include banking, security, insurance, and law, but there are many others. These businesses already exist within a state, but can find added economic growth by moving toward production support.

The biggest challenge for a state is recognizing the economic impact the entertainment industry has on these professions. These businesses will see an increase in jobs and profit, but they may not be counted when measuring the success of the entertainment tax incentives. Productions spend a great deal of money on these areas, and the impact needs to be calculated.

# 10 Courting Hollywood

How does a state build out the entertainment industry in the right way? The first step, of course, is in understanding the industry and creating a competitive incentive plan. Unfortunately, this is where many states stop. They pass an incentives act, set regulations, then sit back and wait for calls from Hollywood that never come. If your state brags about occasional movies that are shot in the state, then the film office isn't doing their job. As Chapter 6 points out, any state without an assembly line of productions constantly moving into the state will not grow out the industry and will not see a positive return on their incentive investment. The primary job of the film office, then, is to develop contacts with the major studios in Hollywood and recruit a steady stream of productions.[1]

How does a film office recruit? Networking is the key, and involves meeting with the right people in the industry – usually in Los Angeles. Like all industries, there is a productive way to recruit and a negative way to recruit. This chapter focuses on those conversations.

## How to Talk to Hollywood

- Do your research first. Find out WHO makes the incentive decision at a studio. At some studios, the person handling incentive decisions is a VP of production; at other studios, the right person may be head of a department. Know who you need to talk to and what they do.
- Understand that this person is very busy. They may ask you to talk with someone else first. They may ask you to send an email. Don't take any of that personally. When they do speak with you, be brief. They generally don't have time for polite chit-chat. Be prepared – know what you plan to say, say what you plan. Be clear and concise. Have your email prepared in advance – it will need to be sent immediately if they request it. Time may be of the essence, just in case they have a specific production in mind.

- Know which movies and TV shows the studio has done. Know what is coming up on their production slate and how your state can help.
- Focus on the business of the industry. Know and use industry terminology correctly and appropriately.
- You are selling your state. Understand what your state can and can't do, as well as what it will and won't do. How committed are your legislators, your governor? Who will promulgate the regulations? How quickly will the incentive request be processed? Who makes the decisions? Be able to answer questions that the decision-maker will ask.
- Understand SEC regulations and how your incentives fit into the big picture.
- Know the infrastructure of your state and be ready to discuss it. Do you have soundstages? Editing facilities? Equipment rentals? Ancillary vendors who can support productions? How deep is the crew in your state? These are concerns the decision-maker will have.
- Be ready to talk about what your film office can do to help. Studio executives appreciate having someone available 24/7 during production to help solve problems. If your office can help clear permits or assist in negotiations with locals, then make sure you voice this.
- Aim for a meeting in the middle of the day. Mornings at the studio are for dealing with yesterday's problems; end of the day is setting up for tomorrow. You'll get more attention if you go in the middle of the day. And it goes without saying – never show up without an appointment.
- Always remember that Hollywood runs on a different time schedule than most industries. You won't hear anything for several months, then suddenly they're ready and they need everything overnight. This is not poor planning on their part – this is the way the industry works. Trying to get the "greenlight" for a picture (studio approval or financial support) can take a while. But once approved, the producers move into warp speed to get the production started. As a film office, you must always be ready.

There are also some things that you shouldn't do when you're trying to recruit at the studio level:

- Don't go in with a picture book of locations. What your state looks like is far less important than what you can provide in the way of incentives and production resources. If the decision-maker chooses to shoot in your state, a locations manager will work with you to find the best locations. This happens much later in the process.
- Don't go in with a list of movies "made" in your state. They already know this. Hollywood is a small community; the person you're

meeting with already knows what previous producers thought about your state, how much support they received, and whether they recommend it. And don't bother talking about small independent films made in your state. The studios understand the difference between apples and oranges.
- Don't talk about movies or television shows made by another studio. This is considered very rude and won't win any friends for your state.
- Don't get all star-struck and gushy during the conversation. Keep a business-like attitude. It's fine to mention a production they did that you admire; it's not okay to fawn over the picture of your favorite star in their office. Stay professional.

## How to Talk to Your State

It's also important to talk successfully with your state as you build out the industry. This primarily involves the press and the politicians. How you frame your narrative will go a long way in showing the value of the incentives – or giving excuses to those who oppose incentives.

- Always report from the positive. Keep a running total of how much production money is being spent in the state. This is easily attained from the budgets turned in to request incentives. However, your numbers should also include money spent by productions that don't receive incentives. Your office should interact with all productions so that this number is attainable. Keep that number front and center – when the press or a politician calls, you've got the right number handy. Don't report how much incentive money was "spent" by the state – always frame the conversation by how much money was brought into the state.
- Keep a running tally of the number of in-state crew members. Most states have an online database of crew members that productions can access. Few film offices use this number to illustrate the jobs created by the industry. Find these numbers and keep up with them in a chart that can show job growth year by year.
- In the same way, keep a running tally of businesses that grow up around the industry. This will probably require working with another government entity, but helps to show the economic impact the incentives are having. Follow up with these companies annually: know how many people they employ, why they started the business, and how they contribute to the entertainment industry. Also keep up with the benefit businesses: look at hotel revenue, security companies, etc. Watch for economic trends in these businesses, especially when productions are in town.

- Each year, compile a comprehensive report on the industry in your state. Show how much production money was spent in the state. Emphasize the growing number of trained crew. Highlight new businesses. A year-by-year analysis will help show industry growth – or show areas where your state needs to improve. Don't depend on economists to defend incentives. Tell your own story – and tell it with the correct numbers to back you up.
- This report can be used with the press or with politicians. As the industry grows – especially with crew and vendors – this report will also help in recruiting productions in Hollywood.

## Conclusion

Entertainment incentives are different from other business incentives in many ways. They are necessary for any state wishing to build out the entertainment industry, but must be used correctly if they are to succeed. States that support sporadic production will not be successful. Instead, the state needs a strong film office that can build bridges with Hollywood and successfully recruit bigger productions. Knowing how to interact with the industry is key to this success.

In the end, entertainment incentives should be good for the production and good for the state. States can build a new industry that provides jobs, new businesses, and a new tax base. Productions benefit by lowering their overall cost. Neither side should say, "I win;" instead, both sides should say, "I benefit." Entertainment incentives will remain the foundation of this industry for the foreseeable future.

## Note

1 See Chapter 6 for a checklist of a successful incentive program.

# Index

For Product Safety Concerns and Information please contact our EU
representative GPSR@taylorandfrancis.com
Taylor & Francis Verlag GmbH, Kaufingerstraße 24, 80331 München, Germany

www.ingramcontent.com/pod-product-compliance
Ingram Content Group UK Ltd.
Pitfield, Milton Keynes, MK11 3LW, UK
UKHW022158190926
475702UK00003B/91
* 9 7 8 1 1 3 8 4 8 9 6 8 4 *